My First Relationship TAROT

Eleanor Hammond, MM

REDFeather
MIND | BODY | SPIRIT

Other Schiffer Books by the Author:

My First Tarot: The Easiest and Most Accurate Tarot Reading That You Can Do.
ISBN: 978-0-7643-5171-6

Other Schiffer Books on Related Subjects:

The Tarot Game. Jude Alexander
ISBN: 978-0-7643-3448-1

The Tarot Wheel: A Fast and Easy Divination System. Jim Edward Lucier
ISBN: 978-0-7643-4439-8

Tarot Tracker: A Year-Long Journey.
Angelo Nasios
ISBN: 978-0-7643-5439-7

Copyright © 2018 by Eleanor Hammond

Library of Congress Control Number: 2017954767

All rights reserved. No part of this work may be reproduced or used in any form or by any means—graphic, electronic, or mechanical, including photocopying or information storage and retrieval systems—without written permission from the publisher.

The scanning, uploading, and distribution of this book or any part thereof via the Internet or any other means without the permission of the publisher is illegal and punishable by law. Please purchase only authorized editions and do not participate in or encourage the electronic piracy of copyrighted materials.

"Red Feather Mind Body Spirit" logo is a registered trademark of Schiffer Publishing, Ltd.

Box and design concepts by Danielle Farmer
Interior layout by Molly Shields

Type set in Davida Bd BT/DIN

ISBN: 978-0-7643-5510-3
Printed in China

Published by Red Feather Mind, Body, Spirit
An imprint of Schiffer Publishing, Ltd.
4880 Lower Valley Road
Atglen, PA 19310
Phone: (610) 593-1777; Fax: (610) 593-2002
E-mail: Info@schifferbooks.com
Web: www.redfeatherpub.com

For our complete selection of fine books on this and related subjects, please visit our website at www.schifferbooks.com. You may also write for a free catalog.

Schiffer Publishing's titles are available at special discounts for bulk purchases for sales promotions or premiums. Special editions, including personalized covers, corporate imprints, and excerpts, can be created in large quantities for special needs. For more information, contact the publisher.

We are always looking for people to write books on new and related subjects. If you have an idea for a book, please contact us at proposals@schifferbooks.com.

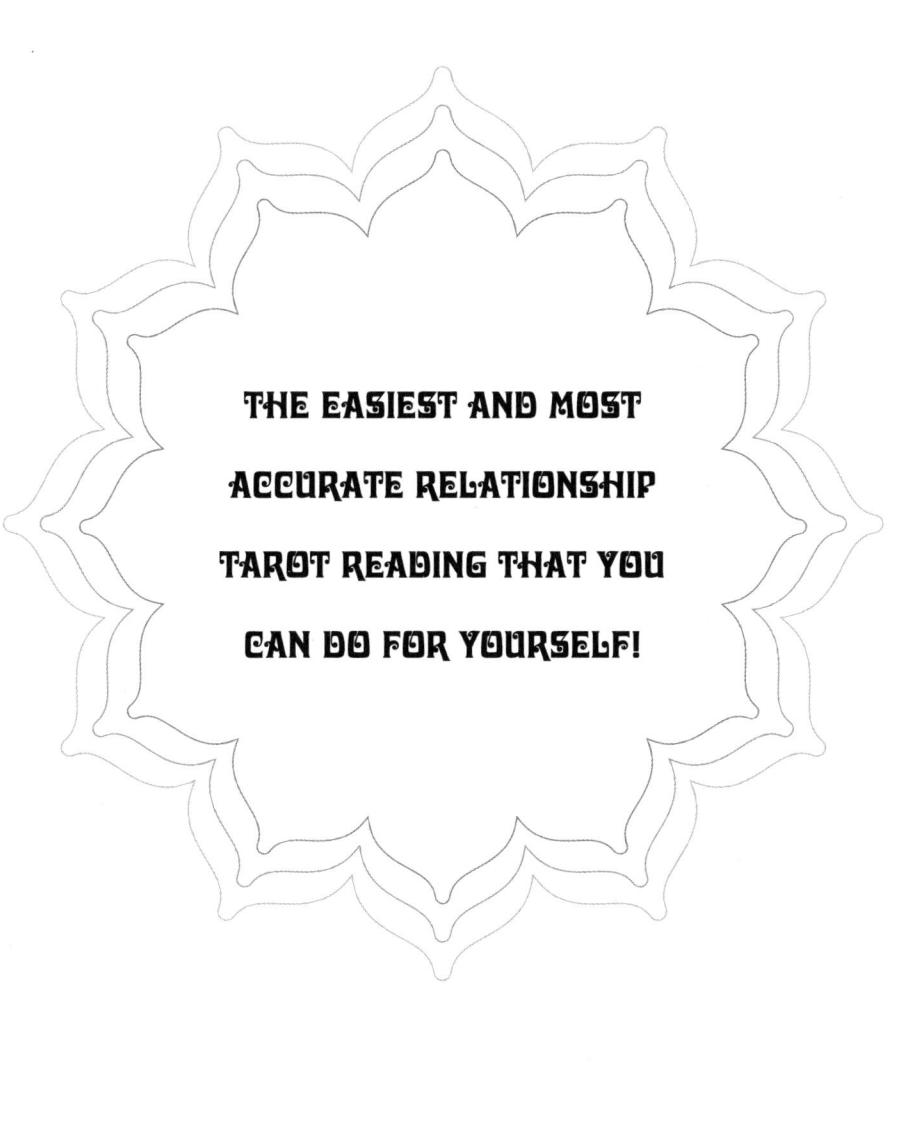

THE EASIEST AND MOST ACCURATE RELATIONSHIP TAROT READING THAT YOU CAN DO FOR YOURSELF!

CONTENTS

Acknowledgments 7
Preface 8
Instructions 9
Card Sections.. 10

The Major Arcana (Major Soul Secrets) 17

0 The Fool 18	11 Strength 26
1 The Magician 18	12 The Hanged Man 27
2 The High Priestess......... 19	13 Death 27
3 The Empress 20	14 Temperance 28
4 The Emperor 21	15 The Devil................. 29
5 The Hierophant 21	16 The Tower................ 29
6 The Lovers 22	17 The Star 30
7 The Chariot................ 23	18 The Moon 31
8 Justice 24	19 The Sun.................. 31
9 The Hermit 25	20 Judgment................ 32
10 The Wheel of Fortune 25	21 The World 33

The Minor Arcana (Minor Soul Secrets)   35

Ace of Cups 36
Two of Cups 36
Three of Cups 36
Four of Cups 37
Five of Cups 37
Six of Cups 38
Seven of Cups 38
Eight of Cups 39
Nine of Cups 39
Ten of Cups 39
Page of Cups 40
Knight of Cups 40
Queen of Cups 40
King of Cups 41

Ace of Pentacles 41
Two of Pentacles 42
Three of Pentacles 42
Four of Pentacles 43
Five of Pentacles 43
Six of Pentacles 44
Seven of Pentacles 44
Eight of Pentacles 45
Nine of Pentacles 45
Ten of Pentacles 46
Page of Pentacles 46
Knight of Pentacles 47
Queen of Pentacles 47
King of Pentacles 47

Ace of Staves 48
Two of Staves 48
Three of Staves 49
Four of Staves 49
Five of Staves 50
Six of Staves 50
Seven of Staves 51
Eight of Staves 51
Nine of Staves 52
Ten of Staves 52
Page of Staves 53
Knight of Staves 54
Queen of Staves 54
King of Staves 55

Ace of Swords 55
Two of Swords 56
Three of Swords 57
Four of Swords 58
Five of Swords 58
Six of Swords 59
Seven of Swords 59
Eight of Swords 60
Nine of Swords 61
Ten of Swords 61
Page of Swords 62
Knight of Swords 63
Queen of Swords 63
King of Swords 64

To Ken, for morning coffees and proof of love every day.

To Jenny, for learning with me to always include "must speak the same language as me" in any manifestation involving love, love being the whole point of this Tarot deck. Words are important folks, make sure you ask for what you want, but make sure you remember to ask also for the obvious, very important things.

To Mally, for your wise words, resonating throughout the years; people need someone to love, something to do, and something to look forward to.

To Ann, for teaching me how to teach, using brutal kindness, true affection, hard work, and bloody toes.

To my ancestors, for sending me wild and magical messages across the aether, proving love is eternal, internal, and flows externally.

To mum, for being silly enough to buy me a typewriter when I was nine, and then showing loving restraint at 3 a.m. Tippity-tap.

To Dr. Wayne Dyer for your calming voice, words, and wisdom imparted to me throughout the years. I, like you, have dedicated my life to creating more peace and harmony in the world.

ACKNOWLEDGMENTS

Thank you Dinah, Chris, Peggy, and Pete of Schiffer Books for continuing to work with me.

Thank you Naomi for the read-throughs and the sensible criticism; Alice and Dianne for helping me get on with the nuts and bolts of life whilst I write.

Ken, as always, thank you for your love, support, and morning cups of coffee, it's now expected by the way, but always appreciated, my darling man.

To everyone who brushes up against me in the margins of their day, thank you; you've helped me to develop, deliver, and make visible my dreams into the world.

... And, of course, Rosie-Belle, for keeping my feet warm whilst I type this, you crazy little doggie.

PREFACE

This deck helps us through the emotional minefield that can be our love relationships. Relationships aren't just love, though; we have a relationship with ourselves, our health, our career, our bosses, our current job, our family, our friends, our enemies, our pets, our living situation, and our financial situation. Just to name a few.

I'm very pleased to present you with this Tarot deck, the second in the series of My First Tarot decks. The first deck entitled *My First Tarot* was published in 2017, by Schiffer Books, and contains a lot more information on every card, because it was designed to give an overall answer to any question.

This deck is standalone—and so is the first one—however, think of it like two games that can work together like snap-in expansion packs. They can be used separately, but together they show much deeper and more expanded messages.

Enjoy, and may this Tarot deck guide you well and give you messages for your highest good.

May blessings dwell in and surround you in all ways, including those of love.

—Eleanor

INSTRUCTIONS

Please look after your Tarot decks.

Tarot decks are made of magic and fluffy unicorns, we all know that, but they're also made of paper and cardboard. They don't like the damp. Now, if they were made out of mermaid hair I'd say storing them in the bathroom is fine, but as they're not, then definitely put them away somewhere safe: away from children's hands, the dog or cat, too much sun, and moisture. I store them in the box they came in, or I wrap them in silk.

Bringing out the Tarot cards and using them should be done when you're in a relaxed mood; and yes, I'm holding in a laugh right now because if you're grabbing the deck, then probably things aren't the best, and these cards will help you to shed some light on what's happening if you do the reading correctly.

Here's how I do a reading to make sure it's accurate:

1. I shuffle the deck quite a bit, and then;
2. I hold the cards and I say a prayer, often a request for higher protection, healing, and only the truth. The prayer I often use is, "Please may I have a reading for my highest good, which is just the truth. Not what I'm worried about, not what I'm hoping for. Just the pure and simple truth as it is for my highest good."
3. Then if you have a further question, you might like to ask it now, out loud, or just silently to yourself. I find that doing a reading for my highest good is always the right way to start.
4. I shuffle the deck another seven times, and I count the shuffles. You might like to shuffle the deck ten times, or draw cards from the middle of the deck; however, I find that if I say to spirit, "I'm going to shuffle seven times," and then I do shuffle seven times, then that allows spirit to work through me to get the cards into the perfect order for my reading for my highest good.
5. Then I lay out the eight-card spread that's showing on the layout map that's included with this deck.
6. Now I read the boxes indicated on the layout map.
7. Once I've jotted down the notes I want to remember or keep, I thank spirit for the messages—even the ones that I don't understand right away—and I store my cards back in the box or wrap them in cloth.
8. I also place selenite, or some other crystal, on my cards. Selenite detaches heaviness, negativity, and also not-very-nice energy of all kinds. You don't need to put a crystal on your cards if you're doing a prayer over them before each reading, but I like to place a crystal on them as an extra boost to the cards. Like putting a little ribbon around a present to someone, a crystal just makes the whole Tarot deck feel more sacred and connected to the Earth, and to me. My preference for crystals is either clear quartz, for clarity in each reading, or selenite, to remove negativity and increase vibration. Why not both?

P.S. No unicorns were harmed in the making of this Tarot deck.

CARD SECTIONS

Each Tarot card has the same format. Each box on each Tarot card has a specific meaning associated with it as shown below:

NAME OF CARD	
OVERALL CARD MEANING	
Who you are, or who you need to be	Background
Recent events	Current
Crossing you	Environment
Advice	Current future

OVERALL CARD MEANING

Each card has a certain meaning, and this is shown at the top under the name of the card.

The base Tarot deck entitled *My First Tarot* shows timeframes; however, you can easily work out timeframes by knowing that Cups is days, Staves is weeks, Swords is months, Pentacles is years, and drawing a major arcana card means that you're not allowed to know a timeframe.

Be aware that timeframes are difficult as they can change when your free will decisions change.

WHO ARE YOU?
(OR WHO DO YOU NEED TO BE?)

Read this box to see who the person being read actually is under their façade. This can describe who the person needs to be for a certain situation. For example, The Empress may show up when the person is asking about their family—The Empress being the nurturer and the provider.

BACKGROUND

Read this to understand what's happened to make you who you are. This can describe what has taken place in the past that is still affecting the person for whom you are reading. If the person were no longer affected by the past, then it wouldn't need to show up in the reading.

RECENT EVENTS

Read this box to see what's recently impacted the person for whom you are reading. If there was a surprise visit from someone from the past, or if someone's just started a new job, or just been married, or had a baby, then they are going to be impacted by this and so will their future.

CURRENT

Read this to see how the person feels about everything that's currently happening. This is how the person feels about their life right now, and it can also indicate what they're doing. It's interesting to see how this card relates to everything around it. Are they happy or unhappy?

CROSSING YOU

Read this box to see what needs to be done right now without delay—even if it's not wanted to be done. You may need to keep studying but really do not want too, or you may need to open your heart and can't stand the thought of doing so.

ENVIRONMENT

Read this box to see what's around the person for whom you are reading. This reflects what is taking place around them. It can be environmental, like a house or work situation, or it can be about the people impacting the person for whom you are reading.

ADVICE

Read this box to see what advice spirit has for the person for whom you are reading. This is a bit like the Crossing You box in that it's also what needs to happen. Taking the advice can actually change the future, which is handy if the future currently looks negative.

CURRENT FUTURE

Read this box for the current future of the person for whom you are reading. If this is bad, then the advice needs to be taken to avert the negative outcome. The future can change daily as the person makes new decisions and changes the path.

Multiple meanings are not shown on the *My First Relationship Tarot* deck; however, they are shown on the base deck, *My First Tarot*. The multiple meanings are not required to get an accurate relationship reading from the cards.

TRY THESE QUICK READINGS

The questions you can ask are endless; below is an idea of what types of questions fit within each box on each Tarot card. Simply ask your question, select one card from the deck, and only read the one box as reflected below:

OVERALL CARD MEANING

Example overall questions:

- What's the current situation?
- Who's involved around me?
- What kind of work should I do?
- What is a job I can go for that matches my soul path?

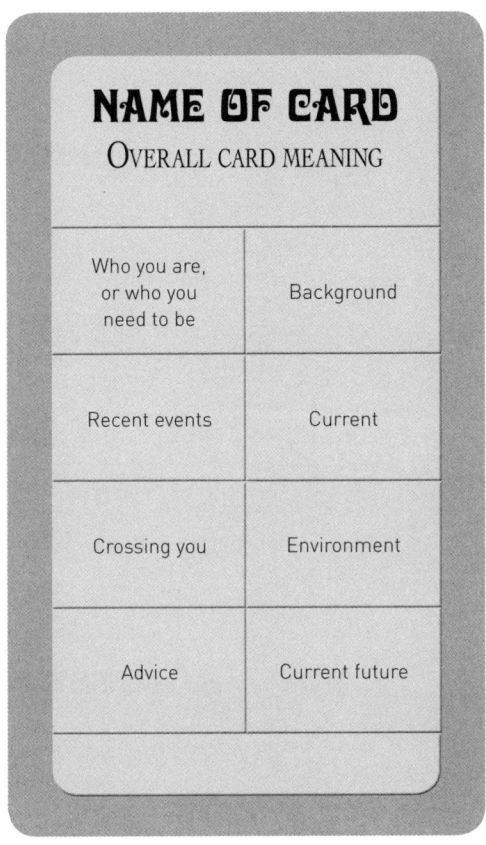

WHO ARE YOU?
(OR WHO DO YOU NEED TO BE?)

- Who do I need to be in this lifetime?
- Who do I need to be in this situation?
- Who are they in this situation?
- Who do they think I am?
- What type of person are they really?

BACKGROUND

- Why are they like that?
- Why can't I move on?
- What haven't I released from my past yet?
- What has happened to them to make them the way they are in this situation?

RECENT EVENTS

- What's happened recently to me?
- What's happened recently to them?
- Why have I changed lately?
- Why have they changed lately?
- What have they been doing lately?

CURRENT

- How do I feel about the current events?
- How do they feel about the current events?
- What's happening now that I need to know?
- What are they doing now?
- How are they feeling about this event?

CROSSING YOU

- I may not want too, but what do I need to do right now about my situation?
- What do they have to do right now?
- What's going to happen next?
- How am I going to cope with what's happening to me next?

ENVIRONMENT

- What is happening in my home?
- Are my friends trustworthy?
- What is happening with my work?
- What needs to happen to my living situation?
- What is my family doing?

ADVICE

- What should I do about my current situation?
- What should they do about their current situation?
- What needs to be known to me now?
- How should I proceed with this new event?
- How should they proceed now?

CURRENT FUTURE

Check for a timeframe on this card.

- If nothing changes in my life, what will happen with my relationship?
- What is the possible future for my career?
- What is their current future?
- What will happen with my life (or friends/work/family) in the future?

THE MAJOR ARCANA
(MAJOR SOUL SECRETS)

0 THE FOOL

When we leap into the unknown it can be incredibly frightening—and also incredibly liberating, freeing, and ultimately life changing. We're always The Fool when we start something new. We can be eighty years old and still act The Fool on occasion, and regardless of age, we can always fall in love.

The Fool is soul's journey starting: either a brand new journey, or a fresh start in a current love relationship, and when that equates to love relationships, The Fool literally translates to "lover's leap." The ultimate leap of faith. This card, being that it is the beginning of the soul's journey, also can indicate a new love, even in the form of a baby, coming into the family.

We leap into love, or are cautious, depending on who we are as people, and this card showing up in a reading can be a warning or solid advice and a big nod from spirit to jump in.

If you're usually a person who is shy about going ahead in a relationship, then The Fool is advice to leap and have faith, but also to be cautious. If, however, you often fall in love very easily, then The Fool showing up is a bit of a sign that spirit wants you to slow it down this time to make sure love lasts.

The picture on The Fool is generally someone who's been drinking wine, dancing next to a cliff, with a dog nipping at his heels. He's usually footloose and fancy-free, able to wander about and live in the moment.

At any stage The Fool can be fool enough to accidentally fall from the cliff—or in joy enough to willingly leap!

When this card shows up in a love reading, then it's time for a fresh start; leap in, but look first, and enjoy the new journey before you.

If in a relationship, then this card may be advice to look at everything with fresh eyes. It advises for both of you to dream of the different ways of living and the unusual ways you can represent your love on the earth plane. For instance, you might be the couple who wants to live on a boat or surrounded by jungle. With this card, look before you leap, but go for it.

If you're looking for love, then this card shows a fresh start, and new love is available to you—but be cautious, happy, and excited about the journey ahead.

I THE MAGICIAN

We can manifest true love now, or we can manifest a love that's shallow and unfeeling, a fake love, not unlike the magician's strings and mirrors act. Looks good from the outside, but has no real substance.

This magus always has all the elements at his, or her, disposal. Earth, Air, Fire, and Water are available to manifest everything that they want to manifest, and not only that, spirit is wanting to help this Magician to manifest here on the earth plane exactly what they want to have happen.

If you're busy asking for a true love that lasts a lifetime, then you have to be ready to look after that manifestation in the same way that buying a boat means you'll have to maintain the boat, and manifesting a car or home means that they also need to be maintained.

In a relationship this card often indicates that you can have the love you want, including a relationship that lasts a lifetime and the ability to keep the current partner indefinitely.

This card also indicates that the power is in your hands and is your choice. As this is a soul card we have to learn to create relationships of value and not just any old relationship that's not worth anything.

What we create is as good as the effort we put in, as usual, and a beautiful relationship created by The Magician can still come undone if work isn't done to maintain the relationship through acting the part of a partner to stick with.

The number 1 of The Magician means that we create at the beginning of the soul's journey. We create something good or empty or lovely or horrible in a relationship, depending on how well we evolve as partners ourselves.

If you are in a happy relationship, then well done; you've made it. You know how to create and keep a happy relationship. If you're in a relationship that's not happy, then this card appearing in a reading is a reminder that we get what we ask for and that we have the power to manifest what happens next.

If you are looking for love, then be careful what you wish for, as this card, like The Star card, is about manifesting in co-creation with spirit. They're listening intently, so make sure you remember to specify you want a partner that lives in the same area you do and speaks the same language!

We've fallen in love with The Fool, and we've manifested a relationship with The Magician, and then comes our first teacher. Instinct and intuition are reflected in the next card: The High Priestess.

2 THE HIGH PRIESTESS

Spirit guides us to continue creating beautiful love connections. Spirit sees us as divine, and as such this card indicates that we're being guided to create love of ourselves as well as reflect that divine love outwards to others around us.

This card reflects that we're all divine beings here on a soul journey. We're meant to meet some people and not others. We're meant to be with some people and not others. It's all divinely guided is the message from this card.

Some people are very in tune with their intuitive nature, and these people tend not to fight the natural flow of their spiritual lives. It will be what it will be, they might say, and float along to the next beautiful connection.

People not in tune with their intuitive natures might fight the energy of this card and will complain: But why can't I have him/her? Or, why is this happening right now in my love life?

With this card turning up in a reading, the answer to everything is simple: Everything happening right now, regardless of whether it's the most beautiful love you've ever experienced or if it is the worst kind, the message is always that what is happening is part of your soul's lessons here on the planet. This doesn't necessarily mean staying in an abusive or hard relationship, as the lesson might be how to let go and move on.

If this card has shown up in your love reading, you're being asked to feel into what you want from the relationship, and ask spirit for help. The same rule applies regardless of whether you are single or are in a relationship, ask spirit for help with your love plans, and then be divinely guided. Meditate and clear your mind of doubts. Understand that the relationship will only come if it's meant to as part of your divine plan here on the planet this time.

3 THE EMPRESS

This card can indicate a female in spirit watching over you and often comes up in readings when someone has lost their beloved mother or grandmother.

The divine feminine shows up in readings when it's time to give unconditional love and support to yourself as well as everyone around you. This card represents the divine heart and the emotions.

It appears in a reading when it's important to embrace the divine feminine, to be the divine goddess, the divine woman, or the divine mother—even if you're a male. The loving support of the divine mother is required from all of us at some stage.

If you are in love with The Empress then you are very lucky indeed, as this person will be supporting and loving for a very long time. Guard against them becoming frustrated and over-tired, as they will give too much of themselves to others. The divine mother, the divine feminine sometimes gives way too much of their time, energy, and love to people, and they can forget about themselves, becoming the martyr, leaving themselves feeling depleted.

When The Empress is in love she's the font of all abundance. She'll provide food, shelter, clothing, and unconditional love to all. This person, if female, can also be a mother, able to fall pregnant and be the divine vessel for a new soul to come onto the planet.

If this card describes you as this person, then it is time to look after yourself. Give yourself unconditional love, make sure you are eating, drinking, and sleeping well, and make sure you're giving love to those around you in a way that doesn't hurt you.

If you are single and looking for love, consider what the Empress does, providing food, shelter, clothing, and love to those around her. She's the Earth and the Earth Mother. She's nature and nurture. So look around you and maybe start having cups of coffee at a new establishment (food), or volunteer at a soup kitchen, or go hunting for new clothes, or help people with housing needs, or join an ecologically minded group.

As you can see, when this card shows up in a reading, all needs are met, and to meet someone you might have to find those people who either provide food, shelter, clothing, or even love; consider a spiritual or friendship group in your area and join in!

If you're in a relationship, then you have an ability to provide so much to others right now, but don't martyr yourself; ensure there's enough time and energy to go around.

THE MAJOR ARCANA
(Major Soul Secrets)

4 THE EMPEROR

This card can indicate a male in spirit watching over you and often comes up in readings when someone has lost their beloved father or grandfather.

The divine masculine shows up in readings when it is time to give support, strength, and commitment to yourself and your needs, as well as to the needs of those around you.

These days the divine masculine represents the mind and how we have to be our own boss occasionally, rather than be held sway by our emotions. The "right thing to do" isn't always the "nice thing to do," and The Emperor is there to help guide you through that process of distinguishing what needs to be done from what feels good or bad.

If you are in love with The Emperor, then you are very lucky indeed, as this person will be supportive and loving for a very long time—exactly the same as The Empress. However, The Emperor is more likely to frustrate you than themselves, as they might like to control you or guide you, all for your greatest good though, just like any wonderful father figure would.

When The Emperor is in love he's the font of all support and loving strength. He'll provide food, shelter, clothing, and love, but mostly to the important people around him. This person, if male, can also be a father, able to make The Empress pregnant and be the divine creator for a new soul to come onto the planet.

If this card describes you as this person, then it is time to make sure you are looking after yourself and those around you from a position of loving strength. Kindness is important to The Emperor, as they know how powerful they are, and how overwhelming their presence can be.

The Emperor can be overwhelming, amazingly supportive, strong willed, and the loving strength and support of a family and, if committed to you, will choose to love you through good and bad for the rest of this lifetime.

If you are looking for love, then go looking for someone who likes to be the boss, or has their own business, or is the master of their trade, or very good at what they do. Consider kicking off your own business, or taking lessons in a martial art, or sports, or in some other area where you can push yourself to be in control of yourself and your environment. Go in search of attaining discipline in a fun and caring environment, and you'll be surprised who you will meet.

5 THE HIEROPHANT

The Emperor and The Empress can have a divine union, which is reflected in The Hierophant. People often mistake The Lovers for the divine union; however, that is explained further in The Lovers section.

The Hierophant can depict a person who is a traditionalist, someone who wants the kind of relationship that was taught to them was the "right relationship" growing up. Of course, this can mean different things to different people, depending on where the person was raised, but the basis of the traditional needs of this person is that they always want to do "the right thing" as much as they can.

If you're in love with The Hierophant, then you're in love with someone who probably wants to take things a little slowly in regard to building the relationship. They'll want to know that the relationship can stand the test of time. When the relationship has been tested and found to be a very deep, true, and abiding love, then they will commit with their entire being—heart and soul.

This card, if not about a person, can be about the commitment of marriage, the entering into of a holy union by two people.

If you're the sort of person who doesn't usually pick the right partners—maybe that means you jump in too quickly—then this card is guidance to make sure of the next person, to take things slowly and build a beautiful, long-term, and stable marriage of souls.

If you are single and looking for love, then drawing this card is a hint to join an established group of people. Perhaps it means to go and study, or start working in a larger organization, or connect to a community support group.

If you are in a relationship that is wobbly, then drawing this card is a signal that you can solidify the relationship in the future.

6 THE LOVERS

This card showing up in a reading almost always means that there are conversations needed between couples, and usually those conversations are the normal, run-of-the-mill chats along the lines of where they are going to live when they retire, or if they are going to get married or have children. You know, the big questions and conversations that we have to have in a relationship. The big "will we" or "won't we" questions.

Sometimes, however, this card can mean a love triangle, or a difficult union, or in some cases, an incredibly beautiful and amazing connection between two people.

Often people ask me when, and if, they'll meet a soulmate and I invariably reply that they no doubt already have. Soulmates are people we can't escape from and who are often our siblings, parents, or children.

A soulmate is someone you agreed to come onto the planet with at the same time, in this physical incarnation, to learn something together. I give the example that if you stabbed someone metaphorically or physically in the heart last lifetime, then this lifetime you might have to make it up to them, so rethink the horrible things you've been saying about your last partner. It's possible things done to you were payback, and therefore karmic in nature. It's a serious thing, though. Learning lessons through connecting with other souls in a predestined way is something I truly believe in, and having a soulmate enter your life can screw up current relationships if you let it.

I have people come for readings who've been happily married for decades, and then they meet a soulmate, and suddenly their world is thrown into chaos. "I don't know what it is about that person!" they'll say to me. "I can't get them out of my head!" It's probably because there was something left over from a last lifetime that wasn't finished or learnt.

THE MAJOR ARCANA
(Major Soul Secrets)

Imagine you meet the love of your life and die suddenly, and then you're both reborn and you don't meet until you're already committed to someone else. How would that feel, to suddenly meet up again and realize that the love you have now might not be as good as the love you could have?

That's what is so hard sometimes with The Lovers energy, the "could have" energy of it all. Should I be with them? Should I leave my partner?

We commit in The Hierophant, and now the relationship is either being challenged because we committed to a soulmate, or we've met a soulmate, or hopefully it's just a confirmation that we're married to a beautiful soul partner.

Either way, the meaning is the same: Realize that the love connections you're making are soul connections, and they've come with a lesson to teach us. We must learn in order to grow, and often love lessons are the most painful.

If you are the rare soul couple that chose to come together this lifetime just to love each other, then that's wonderful; it can be the best love there is. Some people call this the twin flame love, the soul connection to end all soul connections.

Generally though, we don't get married and have children with a soulmate; we come together, or not, in order to attain a major lesson regarding love, and then, after learning, we move on to marriage and children with that person, or we go our separate ways.

This card showing up in a reading can indicate that you are having a baby who is a soul connection to you coming back into your life, or it can indicate that the partner you have now, or the one coming into your life, is a soulmate.

Prepare for the lessons, stay balanced, and keep communicating when this card shows up in a reading. All will be well.

7 THE CHARIOT

The soul journey continues and so does the soul's love journey.

The Chariot showing up in a reading always means that the journey ahead will be fun and successful, no matter which way we choose to go. We can journey happily and choose our direction calmly, knowing that all will be well, and we're destined to do well on the next stage of our life journey.

If you're in a relationship that is going along well, then this card showing up means things will continue to go well in the future. You may even plan a trip or a move, or something to expand the relationship, e.g., engagement, a wedding, a new home, an overseas holiday together, or baby.

If your current relationship is worrying you and you've been trying to decide whether you should stay in it or leave, then having The Chariot turn up in a reading means that it doesn't matter who we choose to love—or if we choose to stay or choose to go. All will be fine in the end. You pick your life path by choosing your life path, so choose calmly.

When standing at the crossroads with love, this card showing up means: Don't worry. Travel and be happy; you're destined for happiness, regardless of what you choose to do next.

If you pick a path, then it automatically becomes your new life path, so don't think that you can't choose a path because it might be the wrong one; if you pick a path, it is already your right soul's path. I know I've said this same thing a couple of times in different ways; it's that important to tell you. If you're worried about what you should do next, then don't worry at all, it doesn't matter. Spirit supports you no matter what you choose to do next.

If you're not at a love crossroads, then you're definitely going on a love journey. Hopefully with a loving and long-term partner to a fabulous and fun destination.

This card always means that inner healing journeys and physical journeys are done together, so if your love relationship hasn't been working, travel together—even if it's just a walk down the road, side-by-side, holding hands.

If you're looking for a love partner, then go on a trip. Journeys to love are now on your life path when this card shows up, and those journeys could just be into your local environment to connect with people there.

8 JUSTICE

This card, more than any other in the Tarot deck, reflects karma. "Karma" is a Sanskrit word meaning "cause and effect," and if this card is drawn today in a relationship reading, then you have to be careful what you say and do, as the result will reflect the energy put in.

To be clear: What you've put into relationships now comes back in a very visible, and probably documented, way.

We may have choices to make with a partner, or between partners, or about what we want to do next, and the decision and how we weigh it matters in the long term. We'll be living with the results for a long time. These decisions are very important, and the Justice card is often depicted by scales to reflect the need to weigh each word and each decision very carefully now. What is done now counts and is often written in stone, or these days, typed, and can often be legally binding. The Justice card is often depicted showing "blind justice," the blindfolded statue holding the scales in one hand and the sword in the other. This statue literally means that the decision will be weighed in the mind of the person making the decision and the outcome will be swift.

If you're in love with someone who demonstrates the energy of the Justice card, then they're usually very fairminded and love to defend and protect others. This is someone who believes in justice and likes to do everything the right way in life. Think police officer, military person, court officer, or someone who prefers to follow a set process with the work that they do; they may even wear a uniform.

Being fair and right is very important when this card shows up, and if there are events happening around a relationship, e.g., a divorce, then it does mean that everything will eventually turn out in a fair and right way for all parties involved. Therefore, if this is the case for you, and you're going through a difficult time, then remember that drawing this card means all will be fair and right in the end.

THE MAJOR ARCANA
(Major Soul Secrets)

Justice in the positive can reflect a need for legal paperwork like marriage certificates, birth certificates, travel visas, home contracts, and other documents connected to cementing relationships.

If you're in a relationship, then hopefully this card showing up means that you're looking to make legally binding, or very strong commitments to each other.

If the relationship is wobbly, however, it can be that you, or both of you, have big decisions to make and to be very serious about those decisions as they impact your entire future.

If you're looking for love, then look to a person in uniform, someone who loves to defend others, or wants to work in a position in life that has a distinct right from wrong. The right person for you may be a lover of process, or doing things the right way.

9 THE HERMIT

Even in long-term happy relationships, we sometimes need our space—some time away to regroup and realign with what we see is important for us personally. I often quote Kahlil Gibran in readings when this card is drawn. In the booklet *The Prophet* he talks about giving your heart, but not into each other's keeping. It's about being the two strong pillars that stand apart and don't lean on each other. Each showing their own strength and each being their own strength.

I'm not quoting Kahlil Gibran directly here, as I'm writing this whilst sitting in the middle of the Australian outback next to a local watering hole in Queensland. Why do I share this right now? Because I needed to be The Hermit for a while. I needed to wander off into the wilderness alone to seek enlightenment. It doesn't mean that I don't love my family; it just means that I needed some space away from home. (It just so happens that my family came with me.)

The Hermit is often depicted holding a lantern and walking a lonely road and can show a lonely traveler or an alone traveler. Big distinction actually: You can be alone and not feel lonely, and you can be in a relationship and feel very lonely indeed.

The Hermit often is rethinking their home or living space and can indicate that partners are wanting to move, or at the very least, redecorate so that they get some more of their own space.

If you're searching for love, then travel alone if you're already planning to, or someone traveling by themselves is coming into your life.

If you're in love with The Hermit, then you'll find that they need to wander off by themselves. It doesn't mean they don't love you; it just means that they need their alone time in order to recharge.

10 THE WHEEL OF FORTUNE

This card shows great opportunities spinning around you, and you can stop the wheel at any time and claim one of those prizes; one of those opportunities is for love. This card, always reflecting the karmic wheel, also symbolizes the need to ensure we don't go around and around in the same love circles that we've done in the past.

If you are in a relationship and it is going wonderfully well, then this card showing up just means that there are great opportunities for both of you. Opportunities could be to create a better and more beautiful love between you, or it could be an opportunity to expand into the world together.

If you are in a relationship that is wobbly, then this card showing up always means that you have to stop going around and around in the same way continuously: the same arguments, the same patterns, the same frustrations, over and over. You get the meaning. This card always means that you have to let the past go and start fresh. Sometimes this means that we can do it together, and sometimes it doesn't and we part.

If you are looking for love, consider the energy of this card. It always means to let the past go and move on, and if you're looking for love, that could obviously mean that you are doing the same things over and over and are getting caught in the same trap of trying to look for love in the same ways. When this card has shown up, look for love outside of your current wheel to see what other opportunities present themselves to connect to beautiful and friendly people.

This is why sometimes this card is known as the second-chance card and can often depict people attempting to rekindle their love anew, even after something as strong and definitive as a divorce—both people more grown up and more aware of themselves and how they can help love blossom.

11 STRENGTH

There are two quite significant cards in the Tarot when it comes to choosing to stay in a relationship or leave it behind. The Wheel of Fortune can mean that you'll be completely fine if you leave a relationship, and the Strength card can mean that you're needing to recommit.

Love is tricky and can make us feel strong or weak. When this card shows up you're being asked to maintain loving, but strongly supportive relationships, with everyone around you.

If you're looking for love, then someone who's a very strong and protective person is probably the right one for you. As this card is connected to the star sign Leo, it can indicate a person who's good with both animals and children. Think of it like this: The lion is the lord of the jungle, and the lord of the jungle in your love life is someone who can watch over you, protect you, growl at you sometimes, hopefully in a good-natured way, and make you tingle with their power.

If you're in love with someone demonstrating the Strength energy, then you've met your match. They can argue with you and win, they can out maneuver you, but you will probably enjoy it. After all, who doesn't love being chased when it's by someone you love? When it's not someone you love, that's a whole different story; if you're being chased by a lion you don't sit still, you go and hide somewhere for a bit. You're not in real danger, but still, better safe than sorry.

Someone who has the Strength card to describe them will be fiercely protective of you and make sure nobody dares come between you. This is one of the reasons why this card can mean commit and don't stuff around, because love can be very strong, but as always, it's a free will decision that ultimately has to be made.

If single, then look for someone who watches over people, places, animals, or children, or someone who loves to protect and support those around them.

If in a relationship, then love is strong and can stand the tests before it.

12 THE HANGED MAN

We all know that sometimes we have to be patient and wait for great love to arrive.

This card usually depicts Odin hanging from the tree of knowledge and comes from the myth of how he hung himself from the Tree of Knowledge for nine days because he was promised the wisdom of the runes. Odin was free to step down from the tree at any stage, one leg was free and both arms were free. He chose to stay in order to get the prize, however. He chose to wait, watch, listen, and learn.

Great patience was rewarded and is the message of this card.

If you are single and this card has been drawn, then it's a solid message that you have to wait and learn soul lessons before great love can enter your life.

As an example, I have seen this message come out in a reading when someone who is in the middle of a course asks the question: should I keep studying or move to be with my new partner? The answer, of course, when this card appears, is that the great prize comes if you can do the study before moving towards your lover. The relationship will be richer and more rewarding, or will fall away and allow something stronger to come in.

If you are in a relationship then drawing this card means patience is going to be rewarded. Be patient with each other now as all things change.

13 DEATH

This card simply means change. Change is scary if we let it be scary.

If we fall in love, that's a change, and that can be both scary and exciting. If we fall pregnant, then there's an immediate and abrupt change in relationships.

When the death card appears in a reading I'm mindful to tell people that it is a soul card, and change is a constant in every life. Our love lives change rapidly from time to time and it's often a beautiful and happy event that occurs with that change. Consider a wedding day, a birthday, a day you walk into your new home. Everything has changed forever after this moment.

Very rarely does this card indicate an ending of a relationship, as it usually means you can have a fast and fresh start within a relationship; however, if you are in a relationship that is ending, drawing this card does indicate that it can happen rapidly if it's for your highest good to have it end quickly. Sometimes it's best for both parties to walk away and not look back.

If you are single and looking for love, this card reflects an ability to have love come in abruptly and unexpectedly. Wow! Did I just meet someone amazing!

A funny story that fits this card is a person left one of my readings and literally had a small collision—two vehicles—and met the person she's now with. She came back in laughing and said, "Hey Eleanor, you didn't give me all the details there when you said I would be running into someone unexpectedly!" We both smiled.

Hopefully you don't have to go to such extremes to find love, but if you're looking, definitely do something unusual, as love is somewhere unexpected. Possibly and unfortunately, even at a funeral. Love, as the saying goes, can pop up when you're definitely not looking for it.

14 TEMPERANCE

When the Temperance card is drawn in a reading, I always tell people that the main message comes from the archetype of Archangel Gabriel, the healer. This card usually shows Archangel Gabriel mixing the medicine of the soul, and as the soul churns and changes, we undergo soul lessons, feel pain or happiness, and we grow. Often the Temperance card is linked to hospitals and healing of all kinds.

Soul lessons can often be painful as pain is one of our teachers here on the planet; however, often the lesson is one of allowing the flow of our lives to change. Holding on sometimes creates pain. Once the soul lessons have been learnt, then the healer is born.

In relationships this card reflects the need for moderation and balance and is often associated with not overdoing anything. Being temperate means to be restrained and well-balanced. We can love gently, talk to each other gently, and we can help to heal the wounds inflicted through the passage of our past loves.

When you're in love with someone who demonstrates the Temperance energy, they'll be nurturing and kind, if they've gone through their healing journey.

If looking for love, then hold your balance, do those things that bring a sense of joy and balance into your life. For instance, you might work in a stagnant job and need to get to the gym and meet someone there, or you might feel that you're not eating well and meet someone amazing at a cooking group.

Occasionally, we're not balanced enough to allow love into our lives as we haven't undergone the healing from past hurts that we need to. Focus on healing on the inside and realize that real love starts there first. As soon as you've got that nailed, you will discover that love of all kinds will quickly follow.

A person that fits this energy may be a nurse, doctor, physiotherapist, counselor, mother, father, a great communicator, someone who lives a balanced approach to life, or someone who seeks to live a balanced life; someone learning to become more balanced. Anybody who seeks to help themselves and others will certainly fit this energy as a potential love partner.

THE MAJOR ARCANA
(Major Soul Secrets)

15 THE DEVIL

Be careful what you sign up for!

This card showing up in a reading often reflects a need for relationships to be set up correctly the first time. The devil's in the details is the saying. If you buy a car, then the car might be a jalopy and continuously break down, or it can be a car that keeps going on the sniff of an oily rag. It's still the purchase of a car.

If you marry a man (or woman) and you're happy, or not so happy, then you've still married that person. It's still a contract that you entered into.

Did you check the details and set up the contract the way that was right? Or didn't you? If you didn't check the details, then you may have ended up committed to someone who doesn't want children when you do, all because you never had the conversation.

We are never truly bound to anyone or anything, regardless of what we might think, and the ultimate trap of the devil energy is that we think we are. We don't make changes because we tell ourselves that we can't make changes. "I committed to this," we say to ourselves and the people around us. I committed to this relationship, and I feel like I now need to stay.

Sometimes the energy is in reverse, and we've wholeheartedly committed and assume that the other person has too. That also hurts.

The Devil card can show commitment, and it can also show temptation. The message is always that we need to take care of the way we set up new relationships so that they remain strong long-term, and the way we do that is by checking the details; we talk to each other. We check what our goals and long-term plans are before we commit—if we can resist the lure of passion for long enough to have the chats, anyway.

The Devil is someone who is passionate, irresistible, and won't commit until ready, but when they do commit, it's fully and completely, and this card can, therefore, indicate marriage and contracts of all kinds.

If you are single, then this card showing up means that someone irresistible is on their way. Prepare to have your life rocked, and make sure you're not lured into being too passionate too quickly. Keep grounded, and take your time to make sure the relationship isn't all passion, but also has real substance.

16 THE TOWER

Strap in and get ready for the ride of your love life when this card shows up in a reading.

If you've been naughty, then this card indicates that your partner will find out, and if you've been good, then this card very plainly means that there's upheaval.

When this card shows up when I'm doing a reading for someone else, I talk about the roller coaster ride of life. Some people love the roller coaster, and they'll go again and again and scream with fun and happiness. Some people hate the roller coaster and will scream for entirely different reasons and wind up being quite stressed and upset from the experience.

The good news is, upheaval is necessary in order to grow on the soul's journey in the same way that the Earth has to be turned in order for a new seed to be planted.

Upheaval can indicate someone coming to visit unexpectedly, or a wedding, birth, death, house change, job change, or anything else that's going to throw your little routine into utter chaos.

If you're in love with someone demonstrating the Tower energy, then prepare for the unexpected. They probably will race into your life skidding and yahooing, or appear suddenly when you're least expecting them.

Let change happen or fight it, the choice is yours. Sometimes love happens at the most inappropriate moments. You might get sacked from a job and think it's the worst thing that could possibly happen, then get a job with the most amazing person you've ever met.

Remember that this is a soul card, and therefore, we may have chosen the chaos to happen at the time that it happens as part of our journey here this lifetime. When this card comes out, it means that chaos is here on purpose to allow us to grow in our soul journey.

17 THE STAR

Be careful what you wish for, you just might get it.

This is the third best card in the deck to me, coming after The World and The Sun, respectively, and it always means hope.

Life can be very good for you now if you wish it to be. All of your wishes can come true, and there's a bunch of gifts from heaven waiting for us to be brave enough to ask for them and receive them.

Spirit is wanting to help you and guide you and support you in loving and surprising ways.

When The Star shows up in our reading it can mean that we're going to receive the love that we've been dreaming of and wishing for. It can also mean that there is hope in an existing relationship, especially if you've been worried. Ask the higher angels, or guides, or whatever your deity of choice is, to protect, guide, and grant you the dreams of your heart.

Often we get told "no" when we ask for something we truly want, but when this card shows up, we do receive if what we've asked for is for our highest good. In fact, it might happen almost immediately.

The gift from heaven can be a person, a happy change in a relationship, or even a child coming into your life.

Open up and receive.

If you're in love with someone demonstrating The Star energy, then you've found someone who's bright, intelligent, and has a sparkly personality. They'll be hopeful, joy-filled, and optimistic for the future.

18 THE MOON

The moon is the ultimate "you're not meant to know" card. There is a very simple reason for this and that is that we as humans here on the planet in this incarnation, are meant to dream. We are meant to hope, do wishful thinking, and dream up a beautiful future for ourselves.

Occasionally, the moon card will symbolize a dream lover or someone who is very dreamy. This card is attached to the Pisces star sign, the sign that is well-known for changing their mind, being dreamy, creative, intuitive, and loving. The moon also symbolizes the divine feminine, that aspect within each person of being loving, serene, and able to birth chaos.

If The Moon card is symbolizing a person you're in love with, then ask them what they're thinking and they may tell you, but it's more likely that they are still dreaming up the future with you. We have free will, and this card reflects the ability to dream up the direction that we are going to travel.

If you are single and this card has been drawn, then you're not meant to know where you're heading in your love life; you are meant to dream up what your love life would be like if it was magical, and see if you can put steps in place to make those circumstances come about.

If you are in a relationship and the moon has appeared in your reading, then it's likely that you're dreaming up a new direction for you both; enjoy the creative process, and yes, it's okay to change your mind.

When people are having issues in relationships and this card is drawn, I always ask them to try and stay calm, and clearly discuss what they want with their partner—if they can, and if they know! If they don't know what they want from the relationship, then try and be calm and clearly discuss their confusion about the fact that they don't know what they want.

Please read The Sun card as well to seek more information about this card's energy.

19 THE SUN

Warmth, happiness, love, and harmony are all aspects of The Sun when this card is drawn in a relationship reading.

All things are known: There is no confusion, harsh reality may be shedding bright illumination over everyone and everything. Though the sun is a star, and the moon is a body that moves around the Earth, in Tarot, they are correlated and mean the opposite of each other.

The Sun means daytime, The Moon means nighttime.

The Sun means everything is clear and easy to understand, The Moon means things are unclear or difficult to understand.

When people are confused, and that confusion clears away, they'll say something like, "Ahhhh, light has dawned!" to indicate that their mind is now illumined. The light bulb over the head was always seen as a bright and new idea in cartoons and comics.

If you're in love with someone who demonstrates this card's energy, then they have loads! Of energy that is. They're warm, loving, and will work with you happily; they want a happy life and are open to having love in their world. They are not suffering from a lot of emotional baggage, as they see themselves as clearly as they see others and the opportunities of the world.

This person can be hot headed occasionally, but not often, as they usually use their energy in some kind of exercise or sport, and they're really too warm and loving to be upset or angry at anyone for long.

To me, this is the second best card in the deck and always means that love will be warm, loving, and supportive.

The only trouble with having someone fabulous enter your life . . . read the next card. . . .

20 JUDGMENT

Do you feel worthy?

The card appears when you're either not sure if you deserve a great love or you are not sure about the relationship situation you're in. The Moon makes things unclear, then The Sun comes out and clears confusion about what we want to do; then we have to decide whether or not we're going to put our love plan into action.

Do we have great love or not? Do we deserve great love or not?

When this card comes up in a reading, I always explain it by saying that if someone goes to heaven, then they're met at the gate by an angel who asks them one question: "Do you feel you deserve to come in?"

We have to decide for ourselves what we will do to serve the highest good in relationships, love, and ourselves. We also have to decide what we deserve in this lifetime—whether it be in relationships or anything else that we do. This card is the ultimate major life-changing decision card and shows up when decisions have to be made. In The Justice card we see the decisions being weighed up; in The Judgment card we now have to decide.

If you are in love with someone who demonstrates this card's energy, then you're in love with someone who can be quite judgmental but generally will make a decision and then stand by it. They will stand by their decision regardless of the outcome.

This is someone who will own up to what they have done wrong or, if they haven't learnt their soul lessons, they will vigorously deny all blame for everything that can possibly be pinned on them. It all depends on whether this person has learnt this lesson or if they are through their soul's journey around judgment this lifetime or not. In the same way that the healer needs first to be healed, the judgmental person needs to judge themselves and learn where their judgment is appropriate—before they're allowed to judge anyone else.

THE MAJOR ARCANA
(Major Soul Secrets)

21 THE WORLD

Yay, you've made it! This card is often a depiction of heaven or having achieved a bunch of sacred goals, and it always means that you've achieved the end of a major soul journey.

When this equates to love, you've achieved a major soul lesson regarding how you give love and how you receive love and a great deal of sacred knowledge about the kind of love you'll allow onto your soul journey from now on.

This is the ultimate "I've reached the end of this journey; I've learnt what I was supposed to learn" card. Therefore, this card, more than any other, can mean the end of a relationship, but only if the relationship was bad for us and was meant to end right now.

I consider this card the best one in the Tarot deck, and it always means that everything has turned out for the highest good of everyone concerned, even if it doesn't feel very good.

If love already in your life is wonderful and this card has shown up, then use the energy coming in to travel the world, expand, love, sing, and be happy. You might both like to do something new and exciting together. Plan a romantic trip, or do something that makes both your minds expand into joyfulness.

If single and looking for love, then that journey is coming to an end. Great love is before you. Start something new: A course, business, travel, or whatever you feel called to do next, love will quickly follow when you choose to be happy and allow yourself to expand out into the world around you.

THE MINOR ARCANA
(MINOR SOUL SECRETS)

ACE OF CUPS

There are three yes's in a Tarot deck—the Ace of Cups, the Two of Cups, and the Nine of Cups—and they all mean a yes to different kinds of questions.

This card indicates that if your wish is based around a fresh start in life, then you can absolutely have one.

If you're asking for new love or a fresh start in a current relationship, then both will be possible for you. Also, if you're asking to expand your home in a state of love, or have a new home in order to feel better about life, then it's also a yes to that spirit request.

A physical body is a new home for a soul and, therefore, this card can indicate a baby is coming into the family.

A new physical house may be a new home for the people within the family; therefore, this card can indicate a new home or the home expanding in love. It can even indicate people moving in together to create the home of the heart.

Spirit will aways expand the heart in a way that's best for the long-term growth of the soul, and even though this card ensures new love will come, it doesn't often indicate a time frame.

TWO OF CUPS

As mentioned, there are three yes's in a Tarot deck, including the Two of Cups, and they all mean a yes to different kinds of questions.

This card indicates that if your wish is based around a union of the soul, then you can absolutely have that, and this card can indicate that people are moving in together, getting married, traveling together, or having fun together.

The Two of Cups is the Two of Hearts, and two hearts together is often the symbol for marriage.

It can mean that we're needing to open up to love and if you're searching for love, it is either already around you or definitely underway. Don't be afraid to commit your heart to someone you love or a path in life that you'd love to be on.

Don't be afraid of the future; plan and look forward to it.

THREE OF CUPS

This card indicates that there are outside influences taking place around a union, it can mean that people are coming together to celebrate with a couple as they marry, and it can also indicate that spirit is bringing in the right person.

Imagine the Three of Cups being like Cupid, the little guy with the wings and the love arrows. You can't see him, and he'll fire that arrow in a surprising way, but it's always good. It's always love.

Sometimes love can be wrong timing or create havoc, but it's still love.

THE MINOR ARCANA
(Minor Soul Secrets)

If searching for love, this card is a reminder to always stay open to receiving a beautiful gift of the heart, and if with a partner, expect an engagement, and if engaged, then the wedding invitations are probably due to go out.

If you're in a relationship that is having problems at the moment, then this card reflects the ability for the love held inside the union to be demonstrated once again. Love can conquer all issues, and unstable relationships can be strong.

FOUR OF CUPS

If this card has shown up and you're in a relationship that's confusing and messy, don't give up on it just yet, it can still right itself and be wonderful.

Often in relationships we feel that things aren't going as well as we would want them to. This card reflects that even though love can be difficult, it's still love and ultimately will go very well indeed. You probably already suspect that though.

If you're searching for a partner, then mix up your social life a bit. Not long-term, but definitely do something to shake yourself up a little bit.

For instance, you might join a volunteer organization to do a cake drive, or go to a fun event, meet new people at garage sales, start an additional and fun job, or go into a contract position for a while. The message is to do something that isn't necessarily stable long-term but that does take you out of your comfort zone for a little while in order to bring new people into your life.

Love is messy and this card reflects the fact that love, at times, needs to be messy in order to grow and change.

FIVE OF CUPS

The Five is in the middle; it's the half-full, half-empty space in a relationship where we're crying over what's missing or lost to us, or we're trying to see what's good and what still remains for our hearts to cling to.

Often this card depicts sadness, but it doesn't have to. It can mean crazy, happy, zany, and very fun times.

Regardless of whether your heart is happy or sad right now, remember with the energy of the Fives, that love is always in transition. We're never perfectly in balance. We sometimes swing a short distance into happy then swing backwards into melancholy. The emotional pendulum helps teach soul lessons about love.

This is all perfectly good, perfectly okay, and perfectly right. If you need to cry, or laugh, then do it now when this card shows up. Allow yourself to feel the emotions that you're holding within, and allow your heart to open and heal.

If you're looking for love, then get out and do something creative and connected to your own heart, e.g., painting, acting, singing, or dancing, or whatever you can do that demonstrates what you love. Allow your emotions to fly free with creative pursuits of all kinds.

SIX OF CUPS

This card is often linked to reunions and thinking about people and places from the past. I call it the waters of remembrance.

This card is a Minor Arcana (Minor Soul Secrets) card that can mean reincarnation and two people coming back together again, even after a lifetime has already passed.

In the Major Arcana (Major Soul Secrets), The Death card can also link to reincarnation, and The Lovers card can link to soulmate relationships; however, the Six of Cups can reflect a reincarnation and getting back together in a new lifetime without the major and messy soul lessons to learn.

Therefore, this card reflects that there can be peace, harmony, and love connected to people entering your life from the past—either a past life or your current past. Consider connecting up again with school friends at a reunion and finding that you actually are interested in that guy who used to be gawky who followed you around in school. You may have not even noticed him back then, but time has moved on, and the zits are no more, his eyes shine, his heart has matured, and he's now a man to be counted upon.

I always say when this card shows up it might be someone from your past that you want back in your life, but not necessarily someone you had a relationship with before—just someone you used to know.

If already in a relationship, then this is a card of anniversaries, reunions, happy times, and great love.

SEVEN OF CUPS

This card coming up in relationships can mean that things aren't going well at the moment, but there's still love. It's the ultimate marriage card, not a wedding card, but a humdrum, beautiful, long-term, frustrating, annoying, but "I still love them" card.

Often this card appears when we're trying too hard to do too many things, and we're wishing we could do better.

Well, folks, give yourselves and each other a break. There's love between you, frustration and disillusionment also maybe, but true love is a series of bumps and kisses better.

You'll be okay. Do the best you can in love as well as in life, don't be too hard on yourself when you don't get everything perfect or right the first time.

When this card appears repeat this mantra: "We're doing the best we can—not as well as we want to be doing, and that's okay."

If looking for love, and having love seems like a fantasy, then this card asks you to look around yourself with fresh eyes and think again.

THE MINOR ARCANA
(Minor Soul Secrets)

EIGHT OF CUPS

Go with the flow. Let go and let God. Surrender and release. Meditate and set your heart free.

All good sayings, all connected to the energy of this card. If this card has shown up in your reading, then you're being asked to let go of anything that doesn't keep your heart and mind at peace, including arguments with yourself, your partner, and what you're doing, and any issues you have with your current love path.

Allow everything to be okay with everything as it is, right now, regardless of outward appearances and regardless of how your love life might be feeling.

Drink water, walk by the beach, be cruisy, go for a bath or swim, don't drink too much alcohol, watch fun movies, play fun games, release any negative feelings from your heart, release negative thoughts from the mind, and flow into a smoother, more relaxed life.

When this card shows up in a reading it's either advice to let go of arguments and go with the flow a bit more, or it's a message that you can surrender your fears and allow yourself to flow into the arms of beautiful love that is definitely coming.

NINE OF CUPS

Remember that there are three yes's in a Tarot deck—the Ace of Cups, the Two of Cups, and the Nine of Cups—and they all mean a yes to different kinds of questions.

This card indicates that your wish can be granted from heaven and is seen as the Minor Arcana card, which has the same meaning as The Star, a Major Arcana card. Both cards mean that wishes can be granted from heaven.

This indicates you having the love you want, regardless of what your question encompasses. If you are asking spirit to help you end a relationship, then that's a yes. If you're asking spirit to help you resolve a current love dilemma, then "no problem"; they're going to give you a hand with that. If you're wishing for a great love to come into your life, even a child to come in, and this card is in your future, then "all good, spirit has that under control!"

But . . . Why is there always a "but"? Spirit will bring everything you wish for, but only if it's for your highest good to do so.

So, relax and ask away for whatever your heart desires; if you're meant to have it, you'll have it. If you're not, then something far better is coming along.

TEN OF CUPS

Long-term happy relationships are available to you when this card shows up. Either you need to be the one choosing the long-term happy relationship whilst you feel utter frustration with the people around you whom you love, or you are the recipient of someone's long-term devotion.

If you're looking for love, then join a community group, and allow love to find you through the crowd.

If you're in a happy relationship already, then expand your heart out to encompass family and friends.

Relationships will stand the test of time and distance, and the only thing to do is trust and keep moving forward.

PAGE OF CUPS

This card is often drawn when there's a child being born but doesn't always mean an actual baby. It can mean that we're the child in a love relationship or that the relationship can be brand new again now.

When we create long-term love and it's still in infancy, then the feelings of childish awe and surprise and fun are present. We become the child of the heart. We feel nervous excitement and get "butterflies in the belly."

Sometimes we're asked to recreate this feeling in longer-term relationships to keep them fresh and interesting.

Regardless of how long we've been together, create a sense of wonder, magic, and mystery, and enjoy.

If single, then open to the magic around you: Get out and feed your inner child; the right person for you might just be the one serving the ice cream.

KNIGHT OF CUPS

Get moving with love when this card shows up in a love reading. Have fun, get motivated, go on exciting journeys together, or consider a journey to find the right love partner.

The Knight of Cups is often depicted as a noble knight on his trusty steed and is often someone who is adored by many. He's the suitor who has a rose between his teeth and charisma to burn. He'll sweep you off your feet and leave you in a pile of dreamy mush in his aftermath.

The good news is, he's not like the dashing knight who comes in and is set to break your heart, usually. Sometimes he is, but not usually.

Usually . . . he's the knight that wants to bring in love, and commit to you, even though you might not think you're worthy of such a knightly figure. You are, if you let yourself, and don't mistrust him.

Just because someone is adored by many and is seen as a fun and exciting person to be around, doesn't mean that they always want lots of attention. They will commit to a person fully when they are in love.

QUEEN OF CUPS

The Queens and Kings are equals. The Queen loves to work with you and the King likes to do things his way.

THE MINOR ARCANA
(Minor Soul Secrets)

The Queen of Cups is the Queen of Hearts and loves to work with you to ensure you're feeling loved by her in all ways.

She's the mother, the lover, the friend, the supporter, and sometimes the drained and exhausted martyr from giving all of her energy to those she loves. Sometimes the Queen of Cups depicts a loving and very supportive man.

When this card shows up in a love reading, you're being asked to be emotionally mature and supportive of everyone, but make sure you don't miss out. Make sure you look after yourself as well.

KING OF CUPS

The King reflects both a potential partner and the end of the Cup journey. The Cups suit is the Hearts suit and when you have become the King of Hearts, then you've attained mastery over your heart. You've mastered love and all the emotions that can indwell in the heart.

The King of Cups is usually a very supportive and loving partner who will do whatever they can to ensure their own happiness and the happiness of everyone they choose to connect to.

They make excellent fathers and don't mind being the center of attention; they're loving and fun and full of good-hearted tenderness.

If you're in love with the king then you're probably used to having lots of people around who also love them, but please don't worry, the King marries the woman he puts on a pedestal and tends to stay faithful.

ACE OF PENTACLES

Aces are always about fresh starts, and as this is the Ace of Pentacles, also called the Ace of Earth, it often indicates a fresh start linked to the elements we need to survive: food, shelter, clothing, and love. One rotation of the Earth takes one year, so the message is always that change and expansion is coming and can take up to a year to develop.

When this card shows up in a reading, then allow fresh energy to come into your heart. Allow yourself to look forward with hope and remember that all good things take time. This Ace is like a seed; a seed can take a while to sprout and even longer to grow into the arms of the sunlight and longer again to bear fruit.

All things will come in time, and this card is an indication that growth is underway. It might be new relationship growth, but it is happening.

If with a current partner, you're able to bring in a fresh energy and expand your love relationship to include a new home, a new job, or even a child.

The expansion of this card can mean that you're thinking of cementing your relationship for the long term. Consider that if you're with someone, then maybe you're becoming engaged. If you're engaged, then maybe you're considering marriage. If married, then you're considering having a child.

If single, then love is coming, and as this is a card of fresh starts and is often linked to new careers, then perhaps finding love is as easy as changing jobs. This card is linked to new beginnings of all kinds that are linked to the Earth—food, shelter, clothing—so any fresh start with any of those might bring love close: a new place to eat, buying paint for your home, shopping for clothes, or giving your coat to someone needy; all things that may bring love closer. However, remember that with the energy of this card, it's going to take time for new love to take root and grow.

TWO OF PENTACLES

Be balanced and tread the middle path.

This is the ultimate yin/yang card and always reminds us that it is not possible to have dark times without a little bit of light, and light times without a little bit of dark. We're asked to look on the bright side and to budget our emotions and clear away anything that no longer serves us.

Hold your balance is the message of this card. Try not to create chaos, and if you're in the middle of making decisions, make sure the outcome will be good for everyone if you can.

In relationships, we sometimes need to hold our balance and make sure that we're not creating pain and emotional heaviness; we need to look after ourselves first to ensure that we're able to help those around us.

This card can reflect that a partner feels unbalanced, and that they're trying to come back into an emotionally calm space.

Sometimes this card means that a love choice is needed—to stay or go, or to choose between a couple of potential partners—however, usually this card just means that you have to be more gentle with the choices you're making in your life. Consider adjusting what you're eating, drinking, the exercise you're undertaking, and whether you're getting enough sleep.

Once you've come back to the basics that your body needs, then you'll be better able to help a partner to come into their balance also.

If looking for a partner, you're being asked to look after yourself first. Looking after yourself will ultimately bring a lover closer when this card is present.

THREE OF PENTACLES

This card often reflects that all is perfect, exactly as it is right now. Picture perfect in fact, which is sometimes why this card is linked to photography and trying to find the perfect house and property deals. Searching for the perfect partner and the perfect relationship.

THE MINOR ARCANA
(Minor Soul Secrets)

The down side to reaching for perfection, however, is that it's impossible. We can try our best and do our best, and we need to remember that there is a perfection in that.

In love, if this card is about you, then try not to be a perfectionist, remember that everyone tries their best, including you. If this card is reflecting a partner, then the same message applies in reverse, they're either trying too hard or they're expecting everything to be perfect.

Be practical, look to the future, create the best love relationship that you can, but don't hope for perfection as it's an impossible target to aim for.

If you're looking for someone to love, then the right person might be right in front of you; true love isn't perfect, but unconditional love always is.

FOUR OF PENTACLES

Going slow and steady in love and expanding a new relationship into a true long-term partnership is the potential when this card is drawn in a reading.

You might feel like there is not enough time to spend on a relationship, or that you haven't enough money to do anything fun together, or that you've been unable to find the right person to give your heart to. This card can indicate a poverty consciousness; a feeling like we don't have enough. We might not have enough love, enough time, enough money; however, when this card is drawn it always means that if you go slowly and steadily towards your dream relationship, then you will get there.

If you're looking for someone to love, then this card asks that you don't feel poverty of the heart. Open your heart and mind to new people and look after yourself. Looking after the basics in life can bring you closer to the love you truly want.

Step into your power and take your time in matters related to love. All things happen at divine right timing, and this card shows us that even love takes time.

FIVE OF PENTACLES

This card often indicates people going backwards and forwards between a couple of different locations or trying to steadily improve their life through efforts; it can indicate shift workers and life feeling okay. Life might not feel fabulous, and not awful, but just okay.

Often this card depicts people wearing rags out in the snow, and the positive side of this in a love reading is that sometimes a trip towards a cold place can bring love closer; even in current relationships, a trip to the snow to cuddle up in front of a fire can rekindle romance. And if single, then the same message still applies: Take your friends somewhere cold and meet some new people whilst away, but make sure you save your pennies beforehand so that you're not left out in the cold whilst everyone spends time inside having a fun time without you.

Love can kindle around you when you look at the people you can help financially, without being financially drained. Consider organizing a food drive or helping out people who are needy through joining a community group.

Often this card is linked to financial issues and people who work in fields related to finance. These people tend to look forward with a five-year plan to create more stability and are a good potential partner for you if this card has shown up in the partner space.

Be grounded and sensible and look to your financial future and security, and others will not have to worry about you opening the door to others feeling happier and more serene being close to you.

This is not the card for wild and passionate love; this is the card for sensible, practical, and steadfast love, which can build as trust and friendship builds—over time.

SIX OF PENTACLES

There is enough love, support, and kindness in the world to be shared amongst us all. There's great love waiting to be found and comes in the form of a great friendship or working contract.

The energy of this card is that to have good people around you, you need to be a good person. "Be a friend to keep a friend" is the saying.

If you're looking for someone to love, then join a group of people who stand up for something or support others. Consider joining a group of liked-minded people in a friendly way, e.g., a sports team like bowling, craft, community groups like Rotary or Lions, or even an art gallery support group if that's the sort of person that you are. Whatever group you join, make sure it links to the kind of people that you'll enjoy being connected with.

Remember, everyone wants to be loved, and everyone truly wants other people to like them, so when making new friends, remember to be a good friend first.

SEVEN OF PENTACLES

Family and friendships, partners and workmates, all relationships require effort, now more than ever.

Work needs to be put into maintaining relationships now, or teams and partners will change. Trying to keep groups and relationships together can be hard work, but the alternative is that partnerships fall apart. Sometimes this isn't a bad thing, but with this card you're being challenged to look at the people already around you, and try to recreate the sense of love, devotion, and friendship with them.

The seven is a merging, changing energy and can also mean that great love is coming through a change of people around you, even a change of people in the workplace or a change of friendships.

THE MINOR ARCANA
(Minor Soul Secrets)

So welcome in those new people at work as one of them may be your perfect match. Read the Eight of Pentacles as well as the energy continues to grow with the Eight.

EIGHT OF PENTACLES

This card always denotes the ability to have your own business and work well helping others, even hands-on help to many people around you.

It can also mean that you find a partner through the workplace, or through a local group, or that you'll be able to have a business with a partner and be very successful.

This is the card of endeavor, so it doesn't mean that everything is necessarily easy to attain or easy to maintain; however, it always means that love is worth the effort.

When this card shows up and you're looking for someone, then maybe look around you at what groups are available locally, what kind of support or helpers are currently already there. These days that can include a friendship circle connected to your local group and created on Facebook. Get out there and look around. If the group is focussed on giving support to people from the local community, then all the better.

If you're with someone now, then this card showing up is a sign that you can work well together; if you do, work at it, together.

NINE OF PENTACLES

When this card shows up, it indicates that you are a person who creates a feeling of safety and security for everyone around you. People are drawn to you, and if you've met someone, you might feel like you've won the lotto.

Thing is, relationships often feel amazing when we're first in them, and therefore, the challenge of this card is to maintain the wonderful relationship long-term.

If the Nine is a windfall, then the Ten of Pentacles is long-term stability, and everyone knows that if you win the lotto, you could spend it all the next day and be broke again, or you can save some finances for the long term.

In the same way, in relationships, we're meant to look after what we've now been granted from heaven, and look after each others' hearts to ensure a stable and long-term, happy relationship ensues.

For now though, this is one of the windfall cards; you're meant to relax, have fun, enjoy the love energy coming in—but as I've mentioned, make sure you look after it and don't take it for granted.

If single, there's not much you need to do to create love, just open up and allow it in. Nines are the completion of cycles, and this Nine shows us that sometimes events can happen without too much help from us. You're meant to feel like you've won at life and love when this card shows up in a love reading. As it's an Earth card, then maybe consider the big challenges of Earth; buying and selling property is linked to this card, and therefore, you might even meet someone connected to real estate who is your perfect match.

TEN OF PENTACLES

You've made it.

This card indicates that you have already been able to create a long-term and stable relationship, or that you're very capable of doing so.

People can rely on you to be strong and stable most of the time (remember the lesson from the Three of Pentacles that none of us are perfect) and that you know how to have a long-term relationship.

You've learnt the lessons of the other numbers in the Pentacles suit to ensure that you can have a happy and stable long-term loving relationship.

If you're looking for someone, then this card indicates that someone may already be around you and has been for a long time; maybe they're just so obvious to you that you don't see them. It can also mean that you're meeting someone new if you're using the energy of the Ten to kick off a whole new adventure.

When you're standing on solid ground, then you can make changes that are sensible and good for your heart, and that's why the Ten is made up of a One of a new beginning and a Zero that indicates the wheel of potential. New developments are available to you in the love arena if you look at solidifying your life through solid and practical changes. Consider building a home and how you meet new people doing something like this, or starting a new career or job. Both will ensure your long-term stability, and both open you up to meeting new people.

PAGE OF PENTACLES

The child of the Pentacles suit, this card is all about fresh starts like the Ace; however, it's about sowing the seeds for change and letting those seeds grow.

Imagine the child of Earth, the seed that's been planted, and the potential that seed holds for the future.

Imagine a burgeoning fresh new relationship, the potential of the relationship, and the ability to have the relationship grow into something beautiful and strong.

Sometimes this card indicates an actual child.

Unfortunately, sometimes this card can also indicate childish behavior—behavior we're not proud of—or those moments when we feel like klutzes, and we feel stupid. Like when we fall in love and we don't know how to be normal in front of someone else.

If this is happening to you, then be calm and release all fear about your future. Relationships always grow over time and, like anything that grows, will probably go through an awkward growing phase.

THE MINOR ARCANA
(Minor Soul Secrets)

KNIGHT OF PENTACLES

Knights in shining armor are always fun, and this particular Knight can improve your life now. This Knight could even be you if the card has fallen into the "you now" position in the card spread, which means you're the one who can improve your life now, even your love life, so get moving.

Regardless of the current love situation, this card always means things are changing, luckily in this case, for the better.

Love is on the move, and your love life can be better, stronger, more stable, and can grow into something amazing over time.

This is the teenager of the Pentacles suit, and therefore, has a lot of energy; however, it's the Earth element so any movement needs to be rock solid. Think before you make changes, and ensure any changes are good for your future.

QUEEN OF PENTACLES

The Queens and Kings are equals. The Queen loves to work with you and the King likes to do things his own way.

The Queen of Pentacles is the Queen of Diamonds (Earth) and loves to work with you to ensure you have enough food, shelter, clothing, and love to support your future growth.

She's the grandmother, the sensible friend, the provider, the businessowner, the master of home and hearth, and sometimes the depleted woman who's given everything away to those she loves. Sometimes the Queen of Pentacles depicts a strong, often stubborn, but very generous man.

When this card shows up in a love reading, you're being asked to be emotionally sensible and very practical. Be your own grandmother, and make sure the daily bread has been cooked, that people are warm and getting enough sleep, and people will be drawn to your down-to-earth practicality and loving heart.

KING OF PENTACLES

The King reflects both a potential partner and the end of the Pentacle journey. The Pentacle suit is the Earth suit and when you have become the King of Earth, then you've attained mastery over your own abundance. You've mastered the ability to create enough money, food, shelter, clothing, and love for yourself and for those around you.

The King of Pentacles is usually a very strong, practical, and loving partner who will do whatever they can to ensure their own physical needs are met, and so are the needs of everyone around them whom they love.

As they are very practical and supportive, and very grounded adults, they're often called the "elder" or the grandfather of the suit, even if depicting a young person or if reflecting a woman.

If single, then consider that you may be too in control to allow someone in right now. You may have amassed great wealth, or a little that you're very proud of, and be scared to let anyone in, just in case they try to take things from you.

If this card is reflecting someone else, then they may be a manager or businessowner and be very busy trying to keep business moving, seeming to have no time to themselves, let alone for a potential new relationship. They're very practical, supportive, and sensible people, however, and will find a way if you've caught their eye.

If in a relationship, then plan for a rock-solid future together, as this card shows that you're both interested in getting closer to the Earth element in a sensible way—perhaps just growing your own food and feeling richer in your connection to Earth together.

ACE OF STAVES

New passion is available to you when the Ace of Staves appears in a reading. The Ace of Fire, which is another name for the Ace of Staves, is linked to massive messages and whole, fresh starts. Think "the burning bush" or the "voice of God" message. This Ace describes the ultimate and unlimited power that is available to you.

This card is always fantastic; however it can indicate a big message is being received, take heed of the cards around it.

The Ace of Staves indicates the unlimited power of creation.

When it comes to relationships, you have to be careful, as new passion can destroy or ignite current relationships. If a relationship is cruising along wonderfully well, then drawing this card is a signal that you can create new passion and energy by starting a business together or doing something creative, or a new hobby, together.

If a relationship is wobbling though, ensure everyone is talking openly and clearly to each other. Make sure that no excess energy is expended when talking to each other, e.g., no yelling.

If you're looking for love, then this card is a sign that someone's coming in with a heap of passion and energy and it's going to be a fun and energizing future available to you both.

TWO OF STAVES

Get fired up about making plans that bring in joyfulness!

As Staves is the Fire suit, and fire is about our passion and enthusiasm for life, this card shows that we can make happy plans and decisions that create fun and passion for our future.

THE MINOR ARCANA
(Minor Soul Secrets)

If you're in a relationship, then plan a trip or fun event, or even consider making small changes to your environment to make the space more romantic or fun.

If you're looking for love, then drawing this card is a sign that you can make little, or massive, physical changes to draw love closer.

Perhaps you're thinking about choosing between restaurants for dinner, or places for a holiday, or deciding what to study, or which sports team to join, or which path to walk today.

Whatever the decision, make it easily and calmly as this card also means that you can make happy plans, not hard plans, for your future, and love is definitely a part of it all.

THREE OF STAVES

This card indicates that you can get on with being personally successful in life whilst being truly awesome. Sing, dance, speak your truth, stand up, and be counted. Have fun and be playful with life, and realize that love is close to you already, within the area that you now live or close to where you're heading.

Love surrounds you when this card shows up, either self-love is finally flowing through you, or a lover comes closer, or, hopefully, both happens.

If you're in a relationship, then laugh, sing, and dance together as you can speak your truth to each other and be passionate without fear.

If you're looking for love, then now is the time to allow your light to shine out into the world. It's okay to be you. Be fully you. Don't hide yourself away anymore. Truth, love, and spiritual support is all available to you.

FOUR OF STAVES

Four is the number of finishing small jobs and tidying up and then starting something new and fresh. When this Four comes up in a relationship reading, being that it's a card of passion and energy, it can often mean that you're actually doing something to create more peace, harmony, and romance in your life.

This card reflects not just planning for change, or hoping for change, but making actual changes, to create romance in your life.

If you're in a relationship, this may include moving in together, planning a trip away together, or doing something romantic. Candlelit dinners, flowers, chocolates, takeaway, and watching movies snuggled on the couch is literally in the cards when this card is drawn around a current relationship.

If the relationship hasn't been going particularly well, then this card indicates that you can easily make the relationship much better. Create the time, the plan, and create more romance!

If seeking love, then romance happens after a move or change of some kind. Look around your current living area, and see if there's something fun you can join in on: gym, sports, dancing, singing class, choir, anything that gives you a spring in your step and allows you to expand into the world around you.

It might be that you're actually leaving a job or house, or even a whole town or city, behind. If that's the case, and you've drawn this card, then you're heading towards love. The changes that you are making are bringing you closer to romance and happiness.

FIVE OF STAVES

Staves is the Fire suit and Fives are "in the middle." So there's passion and energy and fiery natures, and there's not much happening.

A Five is neither good nor bad. A Five is not "wow, life's fabulous," nor is it "life sucks." It's smack bang in the middle of "nothing much happening" territory.

Fives, however, bring the opportunity for change for the better or for the worse, depending on which way you head.

This card showing up in a reading reflects that you're either bored stupid at the never-ending tediousness of your current life, or you're in the middle of jumping through bureaucratic hoops to make your life better. You're making changes, which is good.

When this card shows up in a normal reading, I always say to people, "You have to deal with the normal obstacles of life; it's not stressful, it's just annoying, or boring, e.g., doing the dishes every day."

Relationships fall into this pattern, and sometimes when relationships fall into the annoying little patterns of tedium, it's where the biggest arguments happen. Think about things like, "You've left the toilet seat up again!" And him screaming back, "Well, you left it down again!" Wouldn't that escalate to thrown pots pretty quickly?

The good news with this card is that if you realize that nothing is actually wrong at all, you might be just a little bored or stressed about the little things of life.

If you're in a relationship, be calm. Try not to let all the annoying little struggles of everyday life drag you down. Remember back when him stuffing food into his mouth like he's in a race was actually considered cute to you, have a giggle about life, then allow yourself to be okay.

If you're not in a relationship and you're looking for someone, then you have to make a change. Doing the same thing over and over is just going to create more of you not having someone in your life to love. Create a change, but make sure you still take care of your normal life first.

SIX OF STAVES

If the Four of Staves is romance after a move, and the Five is a need to make those social life changes, then this card is a definite "get off your couch and get moving" card if you're still single.

There are no excuses; get a team around you and have fun. Get competitive. Allow yourself to be challenged. Now's the time; get moving and don't delay any

THE MINOR ARCANA
(Minor Soul Secrets)

more. There are challenges in life, and now it's time to face them. You'll defeat them all in the Seven of Staves, but for now, just be in the mix. The dance mix, the football team mix, the after-work drink mixer ... whatever it is. Get into it.

If you're in a relationship, then there's a saying that fits this card perfectly: "The family that plays together, stays together." Do something together, if working or having a business together, then enjoy it, try not to get too frustrated with each other, and make sure you give each other permission to have fun. Keep the workload balanced in the household as well so that you don't unduly weigh upon each other.

If single, then this card means that love is coming; it's just a little delayed. You're being challenged for some reason. Either you're not in the right social setting, or the right work setting, or you need to take a different path home from work every day.

Take stock of what you do each day, and see if you can shake yourself up a bit, in a healthy, fun, and interactive way.

SEVEN OF STAVES

This card means success in all areas of your life, including love. Sevens often indicate that the people around you are changing and that can include your family and friendship circles; because of this, lots of Sevens in a reading when wanting a child might indicate adoption, or lots of Sevens when asking about a move is actually a move of homes to a different town or city.

Success in business, success at interview, and success at winning the heart of the one you love are all available to you.

When this card shows up and you're in a relationship, make sure you're not being too overpowering with your partner. Allow love to be give and take, and allow your partner to win at life occasionally. You're powerful, and sometimes that can be scary for others, especially those who love you.

If you're not in a relationship then one is underway. You're seen as powerful and passionate by others, and there is nothing that can stop you having love except you. You might scare people off with your power though, so watch that. Relax a bit; realize you're seen as powerful and be gentler. Others will reflect your gentleness back at you, and they'll challenge you if they see you as too powerful.

EIGHT OF STAVES

This is the card for overseas travel, lightning-fast movement and changes, and an ability to do two jobs or two things at once. Basically, when this card shows up, you're going to be busy, busy, busy, and probably too busy to say all three of those "busy's."

If you're with a partner and you're cruising along happily, maybe you're planning an actual trip overseas together, and if so, it's going to be fabulous, but check the other cards as well, as just having "an overseas trip" in the reading doesn't always mean "and coming home without leaving half your body weight in an overseas loo by picking up a stomach bug." I want to put in the grin emoticon right now.

If single and this card shows up in a reading, then hold onto your metaphorical socks because you might end up with two partners at once. Love, fun, heaps of passion, and energy, are all coming in fast. Help the energy of this card by getting out and about. Staves, Wands, and Clubs are made of wood and wood burns, and therefore, this is the Fire suit, and fire is our passion and energy. Use the energy coming in quickly or lose it.

Consider an overseas trip, or taking on an extra job, to bring in that partner sooner rather than later.

NINE OF STAVES

This card reflects that you are good enough for whatever you wish to do this lifetime.

Take back your personal power, and don't let anyone else make you feel unworthy or not good enough. Reclaiming personal power is the message of this card.

When it's a person who you're in love with, sometimes they will react from the perspective of not feeling good enough, and sometimes they'll respond from the perspective of feeling very powerful and strong, and sometimes that can happen all at once.

Consider a person who is not sure about taking steps towards learning to dance, and then they jump in and join a competition just to "stretch" themselves after having four or five classes, as they find out they're actually naturally talented.

If you're in a relationship, then drawing this card in a reading is a reminder to allow the foibles and little annoyances, and be flexible with each other. You're both strong in some ways, and you're both dealing with your own issues. Whatever those issues are, they'll be resolved in a loving way if you allow yourselves to just be human.

If you're not in a relationship, then look around yourself to see what's currently not good enough, and consider getting it fixed. Maybe the mechanic, the plumber, or the painter is single. It could be just getting things fixed and organized allows you to bring people closer to you again, which opens the doors to new love.

TEN OF STAVES

Consider this card the end of the Staves journey, and if this is the end and the Ace is the beginning, then consider the Ten of Staves in this way: If the Ace of Staves is a new idea that's like a stick that you pick up and carry, then as you travel the Staves' journey you pick up more and more sticks, and place each one on your back. By the time you get here, to the Ten, then you've got a heap of heaviness on your back, ten sticks to be exact. It can feel like you've amassed a heap of little burdens, and you can't bear another one! Think "the straw that broke the camel's back" as a saying that might match this card. Basically, you can't possibly fit one more thing into your life. You physically don't have the energy left over for anything new until you've finished what you've started.

THE MINOR ARCANA
(Minor Soul Secrets)

This card coming out in a reading indicates that you are at the end of a physically hard journey, and you can now drop the burdens that you've amassed and start fresh. It's not been a stressful journey, just a tough one. There may have not been a lot to think about, but there was plenty of work to do.

Consider what happens when we move house. You know what you have to do, and it can be stressful, but generally it's just effort. You pack something, move it, unpack it, and repeat until you're finished. It feels like an enormous journey that you'll never finish, but you will. It will happen eventually.

When this card shows up depicting someone you love, then that person is able to carry large burdens. They try to shoulder everything and carry everyone, so make sure you don't become another burden for them to carry. Make sure you help them when and where you can.

The same applies if the Ten of Staves is you! It's okay to get help. This life is a journey and the journey through our love lives can be hard going as well. We can work to create something wonderful together.

If single, then this is the card to get moving with a big project, or work within large groups of people who help each other. Love can be found when you shoulder the burden of responsibility with others.

PAGE OF STAVES

This Page has itchy feet that are tingling with the energy of the sun. This is the Child of Fire, and can indicate someone who's getting ready for traveling or to move on, change their lives, and see what the world has on offer.

When in a relationship, this card showing up reflects a need to do things together that involve using energy; it's not as passionate a traveler as the Knight is, but it is a desire to get moving, to exercise the body, and be passionate about future plans.

If this Page of Staves is the start of a fire, then this card showing up in a reading can indicate someone passionate and energetic is coming into your life.

If single, then this card can show someone who's passionate and has a lot of desire just waiting to come forth.

This Child of Fire is a reminder that we once wanted to skip, jump into mud puddles, sing at the top of our voices, and see what was over the next hill and inside the ant's nest. We might not have been very wise, but we definitely learnt lessons—the hard way . . .

Sometimes, however, the lesson we need to learn, is that it's okay to have childlike desires and passions. Sometimes it's okay to want to look around our world with a hopeful expression of someone who knows that there is no true barriers to success.

If you have energy, hope, and enthusiasm, you can do anything! Including having a passionate and fun partner.

KNIGHT OF STAVES

This Knight of Staves is the Knight of Fire and everyone knows the saying "wild horses couldn't drive me away." The energy is right in that this horse doesn't want to stop running.

This Knight never lets anything stop them, whether male or female—not orders, not borders, not boundaries, and not even their own energy. If they're not feeling up to a challenge, they'll push themselves through until they've achieved what they set out to achieve.

The Knight of Staves continues to run through life until they burn out or they learn to hold their passion in a way that's grounded and practical. Don't expect that yet. The Queen and King of Fire are all over managing passion, but this is still the teenager of the suit who doesn't want to stop, not yet anyway.

It doesn't matter how old you are; you can still demonstrate this young and passionate energy if this card has appeared in your love reading.

This is a person sitting astride a horse that is on fire, baby! Nothing will stop them when they're on a mission. They want to travel, and therefore, this card is often known to reflect someone who could take sports or business adventures overseas and across borders.

If this card has shown up in your love reading, and you are currently single, then either get moving and get motivated, or prepare for someone coming into your life who is both of those things.

If you are in a relationship, consider traveling together rather than putting down roots right now.

When this card shows up it means that there is too much energy for you both to sit still. You both need to burn off energy before you settle down. Travel rather than buy a home right now. Work together to create plans that use energy and are fun. Even if it's biking through France or hiking the glaciers in New Zealand.

QUEEN OF STAVES

The Queens and Kings are equals. The Queen loves to work with you and the King likes to do things his way.

The Queen of Staves is the Queen of Fire and loves to work with you to ensure you're feeling her passion and her love of learning and expansion.

She's the creator, the teacher, the passionate lover, the pregnant woman, the business idea generator, and sometimes the depleted and lackluster person from giving all of her passion and energy to those she loves. Sometimes the Queen of Staves depicts a passionate and loving man.

When this card shows up in a love reading, you're being asked to be mature with your passionate nature, and use your ability to create whatever you want in love in a way that is supportive of everyone, including your own emotional needs.

If single and looking for love, then a person who's a teacher, or midwife, or attached to creating more passion on this planet is the right person for you.

THE MINOR ARCANA
(Minor Soul Secrets)

If you're in a relationship and are female, then be careful if you're not wanting to fall pregnant. You are the creator right now in your relationship. That means that you've mastered your passion and want to work with your partner to create an environment that you can both learn and grow within.

KING OF STAVES

The King reflects both a potential partner and the end of the Staves' journey. The Staves suit is the Fire suit and when you have become the King of Fire, then you've attained mastery over your passions.

You've mastered your fiery nature and know that you can be seen as powerful.

The King of Staves is usually a very passionate and loving partner who will do whatever they can to ensure their own needs are met and that their partners are fulfilled in whatever journey that they wish to take on.

The King of Staves is so passionate that they can make the Queen pregnant, not just with a baby, but with ideas and passion for the future. They make excellent managers and organizers and don't mind putting their muscle where their mouth is. They'll do the dirty work to get the job done.

If single, then this card showing up can mean that you're going to learn something, maybe join a university or become the master in a field of sports or study and meet the right partner doing that study, work, or sports.

If you're in a relationship, then try not to be overpowering with your partner. Allow your passion to simmer and not burn, and show others how to become the master of emotions and energy. Get fit, organize yourself, don't smoke, and use passion-enhancing substances. Master natural energy here on the planet. Tap into your fire!

ACE OF SWORDS

There are three no's in a Tarot deck: the Ace of Swords, the Two of Swords, and the Nine of Swords.

This card is about snap decisions, new energy, and fresh air coming in. It can mean that you'll make a snap decision and sometimes that decision is a clear "no" or a very clear "yes." The reason why it's one of the no's in Tarot is that it's a gentle warning not to make a risky decision. You can say yes to anything, but if you're usually the kind of person who makes rash or risky decisions quickly, then this card is a warning to stop for a bit first, and then maybe scream "yes!" later after you've thought about it all.

When this card reflects a person, then it's a person who's very smart or clever, but they think differently to everyone around them. I often say in readings that this person is easy to spot, because everyone around them will say "six" and they'll be saying "half a dozen." They see life from a different perspective and are usually bravely owning their differences.

This quirkiness is very effective and attractive, and they're the person who will stand out in a crowd who you'll want to get close to very quickly.

Instant and irresistible attraction, sex appeal, falling in love like lightning—it's all the energy of this card.

When this is you, then you're not meant to be like everyone else. You're meant to show others how to own their differences. My daughter would say "fly your freak flag," in whatever form that takes. It could be that you're a very staid, studious, gentle lover who is surrounded by friends who want to go out and get crazy. You could be the person who doesn't drink, so you make sure your friends get home safely, or you could be the person who wants to get out and dance when everyone else wants to sit.

Whatever it is, do it your way. You need to attract the people who are like you; don't fall for the trap that you have to be like other people.

To find the love you truly wish for, be fully your own quirky self and let people see that you value your difference. Let yourself be a breath of fresh air to those around you. When you meet the person who sees the real you and chooses to be with the real you, it'll all be worth it.

TWO OF SWORDS

This card is like a child standing in the middle of a seesaw . . . you move one way, then start to tilt, and come back to center, then move the other way, start to tilt, then come back to center. Eventually you're bored with rocking back and forth and you easily make a decision, thumping the seesaw to the ground one way or the other, whilst you run off down the direction you've chosen. Happy and free-willed.

As mentioned, there are three no's in a Tarot deck: the Ace of Swords, the Two of Swords, and the Nine of Swords. This card is tricky when drawn in a relationship as it can mean that you have two ideas at once, or that you're choosing between partners, or not sure about a partner, or living between two houses. Basically it's a "no" because you could be sitting there shaking your head in frustration right now. If you've got two ideas to bring in great love, then choose calmly, there is no bad decision unless you've not thought it out, then wait for a bit and consider carefully . . . see what I mean? The Two of Swords is not making a decision; it's getting caught between two decisions.

The people who have the Two of Swords energy as their job here on the planet this lifetime are psychologists and/or very good friends. This person can help you when you're stuck and caught in between two places energetically. Think of the friend who helps you figure out if you should stay or go.

"I'm not sure what to do!" we say when we're stuck in this card's energy; however, when this card shows up it's more likely that you need to stop and think before making a calm decision, whereas the Two of Cups is the opposite and can mean that you can flow into loving decisions easily.

THE MINOR ARCANA
(Minor Soul Secrets)

When the Two of Swords shows up and you are single, then someone you already know is a great partner, but then so is someone still coming in! See what I mean? It's not meant to be easy, but it's also not meant to be hard.

If you're in a relationship, then you might be trying to figure out where it's going, or how to wiggle events and homes around to make it right for you both.

Don't worry, be happy, and choose calmly.

THREE OF SWORDS

This is one of the more difficult cards in the Tarot to read, simply because it can actually mean miscommunications.

Therefore, drawing this card in a love reading is a message straight away that you have to be so careful that what you're saying and what others are hearing is the same thing.

Consider someone speaking to someone else who's grown up in a different country and may have a strong accent and not be aware of the little sayings that are prevalent in the former country. In Australia, saying "she'll be right" to a person from overseas will be heard correctly, but a different interpretation is meant to what is potentially received. "She'll be right, mate" is a throwaway remark Australians make when everything will be okay and they're trying to assure the other person that all will be well—even when there's no actual female being discussed. A person from a different culture might just think, "This person is telling me that a female will be okay, and I guess that's a good thing, but it has no bearing on the fact that they're holding a spanner/wrench over my car's engine right now, and before I was told that this mechanic would fix my car for me. Maybe I need to go to a different mechanic right now. This one has their head stuck on a female."

When I traveled to England years ago, I met a fellow who said to me "all right?" to which I responded with, "yes, thanks, loving England." He just paused, then looked at me and said, "You're from Australia, right?" Haha, yes, he was just saying hello, and I'd assumed he was actually asking me a question.

Now think about arguments and how we churn over and over what people have said to us when we're angry at them. We don't wake up at 3:00 a.m. thinking about all the lovely things we want to say to others, but we can wake at 3:00 a.m. and not sleep again because we're so angry over a perceived slight. The trouble is, it might not have been meant the way it was received.

This card can absolutely mean divorce, division, separation, and all the heartbreaking activity that can occur in a relationship, but it all stems from the main meaning of this card: miscommunication.

The miscommunication could be at a long-term level; for instance, take the couple who has been married for years. The wife has always assumed that a husband should take care of finances, and the husband has always assumed that his wife can, and has acted accordingly. The wife is angry that the husband never helps and/

or takes over worrying about money and this leads to many arguments and potentially a separation.

If there's love, there's always a way, and when in a relationship that's strong, this card means to beware of miscommunications, or worse case, see a counselor.

If single, then this is the card for accents and people who speak or have a different context to you . . . or maybe they are the counselor. Maybe they're the person who helps people resolve love issues of all kinds.

If single, then do something different definitely to bring love in as you've been on the wrong path or heading the wrong way to find true love.

FOUR OF SWORDS

Be at peace. Regardless of what's happening in your love life, let peace and harmony reign today, especially when this card shows up in a reading.

When the Four of Swords is a person's job, it's often a person who creates peace or is even someone who helps people rest, retreat, and recover in all ways—from operations in the case of a nurse or doctor, to heartbreak and pain in the case of a counselor. This person is someone who needs peace and harmony and may seem cool and calm in a crisis.

Sometimes this needs to be you when you're waiting for love to appear in your life. Be patient, show how cool you are, not in a coldhearted and unfeeling way but just in a sense that you allow spirit to work in your life in order to bring the right love at the right time to you without you needing to interfere too much in the process.

If single, then this card showing up means that you should rest in the knowledge that all is well and it's appropriate to have some space now. You're allowed to step back and breathe and heal.

If you're in a relationship it's the exact same message. You're allowed to step back, breathe and heal, and allow love to form anew, even in the current relationship.

Rest, retreat if necessary, allow your heart to heal from life's little hurts. Be calm, meditate.

Love is on spirit time, not on our time, always.

FIVE OF SWORDS

You can go anywhere and do anything, even live overseas, or travel back and forth and have many different partners this lifetime.

The trouble with this is: You have many, many choices available to you. This sounds like a blessing, but it can mean that you have a hard time settling down, so if you're young and single, maybe don't settle down just yet; travel safely, live overseas, try different friendships on for size, before making the ultimate decision of future-life partner.

Having many choices available to you can make life very hard, especially if you keep making changes, and it can be even harder if you make no changes at all!

THE MINOR ARCANA
(Minor Soul Secrets)

Sometimes when we can go anywhere and do anything, we feel stuck! We don't know which way to go and what to do. We go into a spin of "should I or shouldn't I?" and that's never good for anyone long-term.

If you're caught in the spin of "where to and what to do next?" then this card is a reminder that you're allowed to do anything, but that you should put thought into it before making the decision. It is an Air card after all, as are all the Swords, which is all about thinking things through, but don't get caught in the stasis of never making up your mind.

SIX OF SWORDS

Thinking scientifically and allowing your mind to fly ahead and fly free! These are all messages of this card. When you're clever and can think your way through obstacles and issues and arguments, then nothing can stop you when you have your mind set on resolving love issues of any kind.

If single, travel and have fun, organize yourself, and allow new friendships to come around you.

This card means conflicts of any kind in your life will resolve over time. So if you're feeling conflicted about being in a relationship, then that will resolve if you think about things scientifically and talk things out from the perspective of being smart and not too emotional.

Therefore, if single, you might feel conflicted about whether or not you want love, or whether or not you're worthy of love, or whether or not love will ever come to you.

The message is simple, whatever the issue is, time will resolve it. Give it a helping hand by getting out and about and being smart about your future.

Fly free, fly through the air, connect with friends, family, and lovers via the internet, phone lines, or other air waves. Be smart and have fun.

SEVEN OF SWORDS

Swords cut through air, and the Seven of Swords is about the way we're thinking and the energy in our bodies. This card reflects a need to be hopeful and courageous and look to the future.

Plan ahead for a great love life, and your plans will come to fruition. This could be planning a honeymoon, planning a wedding, planning for a child, planning to lose weight and feel healthy in order have a future love affair with your own body, or any other plans you may feel are needed.

This card just means: hope for the future.

It's the Minor Arcana card for hope, the Major Arcana card that means the same thing is The Star, the third best card in the deck. The Star always means gifts from heaven if hopeful, and the Seven of Swords always means have hope for the future.

Hope is always appropriate. In any situation or event, hope for the future keeps people motivated and moving forward.

If this card has popped up in a reading and you're in a relationship now, then the message is always "if you're looking forward with hope in your heart, then your partner will too."

If single, then drawing this card means that you're meant to make a happy plan for change to create love and joy around you in the future.

Plan a holiday, a move, a change to your body or home that reflects a joyful and happy existence. If you're not feeling it, then "fake it until you make it." Be joyful and that creates joy around you.

I know some ladies who call themselves the "vibe tribe," and they deliberately make sure that everyone in the group is happy and hopeful regardless of what is happening in their lives.

Looking forward with hope creates happiness in the future.

EIGHT OF SWORDS

Warning, warning! That's what this card can mean; take notice, be healthy, look after yourself, don't do naughty stuff! That includes drugs, alcohol, eating bad food, drinking naughty sugary drinks, and many other things that we humans do to make our bodies and minds not like us very much.

This card is a reflection that things are changing and that there are inner journeys to take place as well as outward changes that can happen.

If you're in a relationship and the relationship is healthy and happy, then this card reflects a need to do your own inner work and let your partner be for a while. It doesn't mean run and don't look back; it means that you have to feel good on the inside before you can show love outwardly.

If in a relationship that seems to just mess with your head constantly, then it's a little nudge to consider if it's the right relationship for you right now, or if you're needing to review and maybe make changes.

If you're looking for love, then this card showing up means that something has to change on the inside first, before love can come into your life. It could be a physical thing; e.g., you're supposed to finish studying, or lose weight, or get rid of the negative inner dialogue that has been attracting either all the wrong partners or no partners at all into your life.

When this card shows up, I go and meditate and make sure I eat and sleep well. Even if just for "that day" as any little thing you do today to help yourself be healthy is worthwhile long-term.

If others around you aren't looking after themselves and are blaming you for that, then remember, people have to want to change. You can't force someone to love you, you can't force someone to be happy, or not to do drugs, or not manipulate, or not smoke, or not believe in what you believe in.

Live and let live, and give unconditional love, even if it's sometimes at a safe and healing distance.

THE MINOR ARCANA
(Minor Soul Secrets)

NINE OF SWORDS

There are three no's in a Tarot deck: the Ace of Swords, the Two of Swords, and the Nine of Swords.

If you are in a relationship and are feeling incredibly frustrated, then this card showing up is a sign that you're not to make changes just yet. You're meant to chill, write down what you want to do, consider carefully your next steps, and think later whether or not you want to stay or go, but only after careful consideration.

If you're not in a relationship and you are looking for one, then this card is like wading hip deep in mud. Sooooo frustrating, but it always means that real love is worth the wait.

Think of it like this: You might be going through life single, lonely, bored, depressed, and everyone around you seems to be getting married, having kids, falling in love, and all-around having a wonderful life as far as you're concerned. You could feel like it's never going to happen for you, and there's no point even trying any more.

Well, guess what? Think again!

When this card shows up I know that everything's pretty slow, or annoying, or depressing *now*, but that will change. It's going to change, and even though you're heading forward slowly, you're still heading forward. You're not going around and around in circles, you're going in a straight line towards the life you want and the love you want.

A person who is single and watches her friend go through falling in love, breaking up, falling in love again, breaking up again, and learns so many lessons from watching other people go through all the emotional hardship, that when it's their turn, they appreciate the gift that love is, fully.

When this card shows up it's a sign that you're meant to learn from watching others try and sometimes fail, and it's also a warning that when love does finally show up, appreciate it fully. In other words, don't just throw it away; work at it.

TEN OF SWORDS

This card reflects the end of a mentally challenging journey. The Ten is a card of responsibility and of finishing a journey, and the Swords suit is connected to thoughts, plans, the spirit world, and the energy within the body.

This card can reflect someone who's thoughtful, and often an intellectual, who can seem cold-hearted.

This is the card for stressful situations as it is connected to, "Argh! I've got too many things to think about!"

When this card shows up and it's about a person, then that person is either a big thinker or very stressed. When it comes up about a situation, then you're needing to think your way through it; write notes to avoid stress.

This card has shown up in readings when a family has fallen apart and family court cases are involved. It's shown up when someone's finished a massive journey of study and is about to do final exams before a big holiday.

The end of a mentally challenging journey isn't that bad and often does come up when life is good, but you're still stressed; consider planning a wedding or preparing for the birth of twins! Both babies and weddings are beautiful events, but no less stressful than any other big event to organize or live through.

If single and this card has been drawn, then don't worry; someone is coming who's going to heal your heart, and you'll heal theirs, too. When two people come together and have either been waiting a long time for each other, or have come a long way to be together, then the love that is found is worth the wait.

PAGE OF SWORDS

The Page of Swords is often, to me, the "child with a knife." It's also the "hidden child" or the "holder of secrets" and can indicate a child in spirit or someone who doesn't know how to communicate very well. This person can also be charismatic and very witty and fun to be around.

This is a person who needs to be incredibly truthful, honest, careful with what they say, and the teacher of other adults regarding how to behave.

Consider two kings at war, their mighty armies laid out around them, and tough soldiers guarding the borders of each camp. In this scenario, the Page of Swords is the man bearing the white flag of truce and the messages to be carried from one king to the other and vice versa. Everybody lets this person through; everybody trusts them. This person knows where everybody is, including both kings.

Now consider the intention of this person.

If they were clever and witty, then they may change the message to create war or peace, depending on their mood and what they want to do. Nobody would know they'd done it. They could create war or peace with a flick of their wit.

This person could, however, be instead a kind-hearted, loyal holder of secrets, who just wants to carry the messages with nobody seeing them, entrusted with the secrets of both kings and proud to do a good job.

Now imagine this is actually a child, someone who's still growing and learning. Are they playing with boundaries for themselves or others? Do they like to "get away with" things that are a little wrong?

Consider the child who pinches a cookie after they've been told not to. That's not too bad, is it? Now imagine this same child is now grown into a fifty-year-old man, who's never learnt right from wrong, and who's been married for thirty years, and they've just met someone stunningly sexy who's interested in being with them.

Would you trust them?

It's always good and right to trust the child, depending on how old that childish person actually is, though.

The Page of Swords is someone who either keeps things hidden, or and more likely, is unable to communicate effectively. They could very well appear sneaky just because they are quiet and witty.

If the person indicated by this card has learnt the life lesson wrapped up around this card's archetype, then they'll be honorable and very trustworthy, having learnt

THE MINOR ARCANA
(Minor Soul Secrets)

early on the benefits of having other people's trust. They make great ambassadors or spies, depending again on which side of the fence they've fallen upon.

If you are single, then be careful that the next person you meet is actually single and not cleverly hiding all the details—those details being a wife and seven children, two dogs, and a mortgage! Don't write them off if they appear like they're not telling you everything, though; they might just not be great at communication.

KNIGHT OF SWORDS

The Knight of Swords is the Knight of clever thinking and may be quicker to move and less thoughtful and world-weary as the Queen and King of this same suit.

The Knight likes to plan for, and then undertake, big projects and shifts and moves of all kinds.

Regardless of whether this is depicting a man or a woman, this Knight is able to consider their current love life and then think of changes to make it better.

If with someone, this Knight likes to make long-term plans, and one of the things this prince will say is, "Where shall we holiday next year?" or "Maybe we should consider moving towns at the end of next year."

The Swords suit, being the Air suit, does mean that this Knight is the most thoughtful out of all of the Knights in the Tarot; however, they're still a knight—open and impetuous on occasion, wanting love and unconditional support from those around them.

If single, then expect a person to come into your life who seems imperious and intellectual, but who is actually suffering a little from a desire to be loved exactly as they are.

QUEEN OF SWORDS

There's a saying, and the saying goes: "People need someone to love, something to do, and something to look forward to in order to be happy."

The Queen and King of Swords are both planners. They like to create the "something to look forward to." They create the future plan and often have good ideas for the future.

As Swords is the suit that describes mental processes, the Queen can be seen as cutting or cold-hearted, but she's not. The Queen wants to work with others, not against them, but is a very clear thinker, and sometimes this can seem like they're all about what they think and not how they feel.

Even on holidays the Queen of Swords will be thinking about what to do next and where to go next, and that's okay—the world needs forward thinkers.

Don't assume that the Queen of Swords is unfeeling. She's incredibly loving and kind-hearted, although she's more about where the relationship is heading than what's happening now.

The Queen of Swords is often a very loving, smart woman but can also indicate a loving but sensible man.

When love doesn't work the way this Queen wants it to, and that happens over a long time, then the Queen of Swords can become a little bitter. It's the dream of the future constantly not working out that can impact this person.

If you're in love with the Queen of Swords, then this person needs to be able to dream and plan for the future, and some of those plans need to come to fruition. When you love a Queen of Swords, get used to hearing them say, "Let's make a plan," or "This place is awesome, but let's think about where we'll go on the next holiday."

If you're in a love battle with the Queen of Swords, then be prepared for witty and cutting dialogue. The only way to win is to realize that this Queen uses witty and cutting words to protect their hearts, as they're softer and more gentle than they let people see.

Admire them, respect them, and be very gentle and kind with them, even if they use harsh words. It's a test to see if you are kind enough for them to drop their boundaries.

KING OF SWORDS

Like the Queen, the King of Swords likes to plan ahead and can appear cold-hearted on occasion. The King of Swords likes to be the specialist and likes to know what they're talking about, even in love; because of this they can seem like they're a "know-it-all" or someone who lords over others. When fully committed, they're a caring lover who's interested in what you're thinking, rather than what you're feeling. If you're interested in someone witty, then they can absolutely be witty, to the point of being cutting with their humor, so expect some cynical observations and hilariously insightful conversations.

Often when the King of Swords is in the environment in a love reading, it's because people are seeing a solicitor, and that's not usually good news in a relationship. It's not always bad, though, as the King signs peace treaties of all kinds, and sometimes the King of Swords is around because love contracts are being drawn up.

Love contracts can include pre-nuptial agreements, marriage contracts, divorces, and any other contract that involves the creation of or pulling down of a relationship.

The King of Swords is the person to see if you're wanting to distance yourself from the emotions of a relationship, and you're wanting to think clearly and move forward with a good strategy in hand.

When you're in love with the King of Swords, be prepared for mental challenges and intellectual conversations. They'll keep you interested and you'll probably learn something fresh and new, which can be very sexy indeed.